THE
PROSPERING
POWER
OF
LOVE

12/25/07

Dear Sas,

Sometimes we have to be reminded that
all things are possible. Catherine Ponder's
books always reminds me of this
simple truth. Hope you enjoy
the book!

Love,
Jett

THE
PROSPERING
POWER
OF
LOVE

Catherine Ponder

 **DeVorss Publications**

ISBN10: 0875168205
ISBN13: 9780875168203
Library of Congress Catalog Card Number: 2006921861

DeVorss & Company, Publisher
P. O. Box 1389
Camarillo, CA 93011-1389
www.devorss.com

Printed in The United States of America

CONTENTS

PART II
SPECIAL METHODS OF LOVE

PART III
SPECIAL LESSONS IN LOVE
From My Three Mothers

The Two Who Wanted Me and the One Who Did Not

INTRODUCTION

THE MULTIFACETED POWER OF LOVE

A Special Message from the Author

Much of the material in this book was first published as a series of articles in the early 1960s. I shall always be grateful to the late James A. Decker, my long-time editor, for putting the material together and titling it for its publication in 1966 by Unity Books. Since that time it has been one of my most popular works.

The early reports I received from those studying this book included that of a businesswoman in Kansas City, Missouri, who told me she was healed of a painful back condition as she learned to call daily on divine love.

Another early report was from a businesswomen's group in Michigan that decided to spend some time at their meetings affirming divine love for the club and its members.

Within a short time, several of those middle-aged women got married! One career woman had been widowed for twenty-five years, yet she soon went off to Southern California to live with her new husband in a beautiful home near the ocean.

As for the club—so many women in that group got married that they had to reorganize the whole club!

I am grateful to the officials of Unity School for allowing me now to update much of the original 1966 book, to add several additional chapters, and to have it republished by my California publisher, so it may reach an ever-growing readership.

HAPPINESS REPORTS

Of all of the self-help books I have written in the past several decades, *The Prospering Power of Love* is the one I have most often recommended—*first,* to people who are beginning their inspirational search; *second,* to people with human relations problems, which almost everyone experiences on occasion as a part of their growth into greater understanding; and *third,* to people who are looking for a book containing a simple yet inspirational approach they can share with others as a means of help.

The reports I have received from my readers over the years on love's prospering power have been multifaceted:

Past-Due Accounts Are Paid in Alabama: I have been working on the collection of past-due accounts by using the ideas from *The Prospering Power of Love*. The first results came last night when a young man brought me five $100 bills!

From a Mental Hospital to a New Life in New York: My mother gave me *The Prospering Power of Love* at a time when I was in a mental hospital. I had gone through many tribulations: divorce, a missing child, and paralysis, to name a few. One minister said I had experienced more in thirty years than most people had experienced by age ninety.

I am now out of the hospital and employed. I have my child with me, and I can walk again after the paralysis. We are living nicely and planning to buy a home. I have been told by doctors that I am one of the strongest people they have ever met. I am optimistic about my future as I continue to study my worn, coffee-stained copy of that book. We have come a long way together!

Taking Charge after Depression and Pain in the Deep South: I gave a tenant, who had gotten behind in her rent payments, a copy of *The Prospering Power of Love*. Since she was financially desperate, she was receptive to that book. She was also deeply touched that anyone cared what happened to her. So she began to declare that divine love was at work in her life.

She had been in constant pain and was bleeding. Surgery had been recommended as the only cure. As she began to call on divine love to help her, the pain and bleeding stopped. The depression lifted, she began making business decisions again, and even went on a diet to lose weight.

Thanks to the power of divine love, she is beginning to take charge of her life, rather than continuing to feel that she is the helpless victim of circumstances. I rejoice that the miracle of love is at work, and I marvel at the changes that are taking place within and around her.

Romance Comes to a Senior Citizen in England: I have been studying *The Prospering Power of Love* and, out of the blue, love has come in the form of a gentleman of my age (72 years). He is a widower and financially comfortable. It is his companionship that is so wonderful. I shall always bless that book for the happiness its study has brought into my life.

HOW THESE IDEAS
HELPED THE AUTHOR

I am grateful for the way the prospering power of love has expanded my understanding and my life since I first wrote about it.

Much of the material in this book was originally written in the early 1960s while I was living in an apartment overlooking the University of Texas in Austin, where my husband taught. We had recently married and that was an especially happy time for me. However, before my articles on the subject had been published in book form, my husband had passed on suddenly and unexpectedly. Love no longer seemed so much a many-splendored thing as a many-splintered one.

"First comes illumination, then comes initiation, after which comes the harvest of new good," wrote a mystic of old. I had earlier learned and written about the power of divine love. That had been a period of illumination about love for me. Now, perhaps, I was receiving a deeper initiation in love in my own life.

During much of the rest of that decade I had an opportunity to live with the ideas in this book. They were a comfort, a companion, and a guide to me. During that period, I wrote chapters on divine love in several other books.* It was also during that decade that I began to lecture extensively all over the United States. A copy of *The Prospering Power of Love* usually accompanied me on those trips into the heat or cold, on long flights, in strange cities, and while I worked with new people in unfamiliar surroundings.

But the inworking is always followed by the outworking. In 1970 happy changes came in my life that led to a move to San Antonio, Texas. This was another especially memorable period since it was there that I soon remarried, and my husband provided me with my first home. A few years later we made a move I had long thought about—to Palm Desert, California—where I continued with my by-now global work. We settled in the Old Movie Colony neighborhood of Palm Springs, an area filled with tropical beauty. There I began to write a series of new books and, at my husband's insistence, to lead a more normal and balanced life than I had known before. (He also has now passed on.)

Further expansion has come gradually in my work and lifestyle in the years that have followed, and I trust there will be greater progress in the future. How-

---

* See *The Dynamic Laws of Prosperity, The Healing Secrets of the Ages, Open Your Mind to Prosperity,* and *The Dynamic Laws of Healing.*

ever, I find that regardless of my life circumstances—bitter or sweet, meager or comfortable—the ideas contained in these pages continue to apply.

Over the years, when people have described every conceivable type of problem to me, I have often found myself suggesting that they study *The Prospering Power of Love.*

Why?

Because as Gandhi once said, "Throughout history, the way of love and truth has always won."

THE AUTHOR'S INVITATION

A Missouri businessman recently wrote:

> I was drawn into the Truth Movement many years ago through *The Prospering Power of Love.* I have studied it often and given away more copies than I can remember. When I started applying the ideas it contains, first I changed. Then my life changed. I am happy to report that my life has vastly improved over the years.

As for what to do with the ideas you find in and apply from this book, a California businessman made this suggestion:

> Here is a statement that has meant a great deal to me over the years: "Love wasn't put in your heart to stay. Love isn't love until you give it away."

Since divine love is a prospering, enlightening, harmonizing, healing power, I trust that your study of this book will bless your life in many ways. As it does so, I invite you to write and share with me the unfoldment of your own unique "love story."

Catherine Ponder
P.O. Drawer 1278
Palm Desert, CA 92261 USA

Part I

THE RESURRECTING
POWER OF LOVE

THE MIRACLE OF LOVE

— Chapter 1 —

Several years ago a businessman pointed out to me the success power of love. At the time, I was writing a series of prosperity articles. Hearing of my project, this stockbroker asked, "What do you have in your series about love?"

Startled, I replied: "About love? This series is on prosperity."

"I know," he said. "But it won't be complete without an article on the prosperity law of love and good will. *Love is the greatest success power there is.*"

Then he told me how he had developed his own private success formula for "straightening out" troublesome people. He stated that when he became quiet and blessed them with an affirmation on love, it was as though an electric force was generated, to which they became attuned. Usually they responded quickly with harmonious attitudes and behavior. If not, further affirmations on love invariably produced harmonious results.

In recent times, we have heard much about the success power of love. A noted psychiatrist has stated that the greatest human need is the need for love, and that none of us can survive without it. People must have love in their lives in some form or they will perish. Love is the greatest power on earth, he states.

There is nothing new about these ideas on the power of love. It was the Master Psychologist of the ages who informed the lawyer that love was the greatest of all the commandments. Paul, one of the world's great intellectuals and a builder of early Christianity, also ascribed all power to love.

You are probably familiar with Henry Drummond's famous essay on love, in which he writes about Paul's epistle to the Corinthians (1 Corinthians 13). In his essay, Drummond describes love as "the supreme gift," "the supreme good."

He says:

> The final test of religion . . . is not religiousness, but love. . . . You will find as you look back upon your life that the moments that stand out, the moments when you have really lived, are the moments when you have done things in a spirit of love.

Drummond then describes the various aspects of love in Paul's epistle as patience, kindness, generosity, humility, courtesy, unselfishness, good temper, guilelessness, and sincerity. He tells of how *a man read Paul's writings on love once a week for three months, and how this changed his whole life.*

PERSONAL AND IMPERSONAL LOVE

You and I might think of love in the terms Paul uses to describe it. We can express these qualities both as personal love and as impersonal love. Personal love could be expressed as *kindness*, *tenderness*, *courtesy*, *affection*, *approval*, *consideration*, *appreciation*, and *devotion* to those in our family groups. Impersonal love is basically the ability to get along with people, without personal attachment or emotional involvement. "I LOVE ALL PEOPLE AND ALL PEOPLE LOVE ME, WITHOUT ATTACHMENT" is a fine statement to use often in developing a consciousness of impersonal love and good will toward business associates and toward those with whom we interact in our workaday world.

LOVE SOLVES BOTH
PERSONAL AND BUSINESS PROBLEMS

I know of a group of persons who once experimented with the power of love in a prayer group and found it to be the greatest thing in the world for solving both personal and business problems. Once a week these persons met for an hour and affirmed statements of divine love. They brought to these meetings their private prayer lists of people and situations they wished to bless with the success power of love. No one else saw their prayer lists, nor did they talk about the people and problems their prayer lists represented.

Instead, they quietly placed their hands on their individual prayer lists while they affirmed together

various statements on divine love. "DIVINE LOVE IS
DOING ITS PERFECT WORK IN ME AND THROUGH ME
NOW" they affirmed for themselves, for their own
health, wealth, and happiness. "DIVINE LOVE IS
DOING ITS PERFECT WORK IN YOU AND THROUGH YOU
NOW" they affirmed for those on their prayer lists.

For a number of weeks they met and affirmed
statements of love over and over. In a quiet way,
amazing things began to happen to the various members of that group and to the people for whom they
prayed. One businesswoman was out of harmony with
a number of her friends. As she began dwelling on
affirmations of love, her friends began appearing unexpectedly at the prayer group meetings, and reconciliation quickly took place.

Another businesswoman had been troubled for
some time because of a misunderstanding that had
arisen months previously between her and some
friends. She had made every effort to apologize and
bring about harmony and understanding again, but
she had been coldly rebuffed in spite of her letters,
telephone calls, and personal contacts.

One night during the regular prayer time as the
group was affirming divine love for the names on the
prayer lists, this woman and one other woman in the
group both heard a popping noise in the air. The other
woman discounted it, thinking it to be only her
imagination. But after the meeting concluded, the
businesswoman came to her and confidentially said:
"Did you hear that popping sound in the air? That
wasn't your imagination. It really happened! That was
the hard thoughts that have existed between me and
my friends. I'm convinced that tonight, through our

spoken words, divine love dissolved the hard thoughts and disharmony that existed between us. That was the dissolving power of love you heard, healing that situation!"

From that night on she had a completely different feeling about the situation. She felt peaceful and harmonious. She quietly gave thanks that divine understanding had been established and that divine love had helped resolve the previous misunderstanding and hostility.

Some weeks later, though no outer change had come, she felt led to contact her friends again. This time, instead of rebuffing her, they reacted as though nothing had ever been wrong between them. The previous cordiality, understanding, and friendship were reestablished and continue even now.

LOVE IS WITHIN YOU

Perhaps you do not have access to such a prayer group. You can still experience the success power of love. You have all the love you need for healing, prosperity, and happy human relationships right *within* yourself. Divine love is one of your mental and spiritual faculties. *You do not have to search outside yourself for love. You can begin releasing it from within outward, through your thoughts, words, actions, and affirmative prayers.* As you do, you will experience the success power of love in all its fullness, as it works through people, situations, and conditions that concern you.

A world-renowned sociologist once conducted research studies at Harvard University on the power of love. Under his direction, a staff of scientists studied love. Their findings were that *love, like other good things, can be produced deliberately by human beings.* They stated that there is no reason why we cannot learn to generate love as we do other natural forces.

Thus there is no reason for you to feel disillusioned or disappointed if love has seemingly let you down or passed you by. Those who bitterly declare that their lives are without love are mistakenly looking to someone or something outside themselves for love. Begin realizing now that love is first *within* you and can be released through your thoughts, feelings, words, and actions. As you begin developing love from within outward, you are truly proving that your method is spiritual, scientific, and satisfying. You no longer feel at the mercy of people, situations, and conditions. You become master of your world and free from hurt, fear, disappointment, and disillusionment.

It is like developing an electric force. Love will begin to radiate outwardly into every part of your world, to attract to you the right people, situations, and conditions that will add to your success and happiness. You will soon realize that instead of your being at the mercy of the world, the world responds to your own thoughts and feelings; and that when your thoughts and feelings generate love, the world about you will happily respond in a most wonderful way! This is the success power of love.

THE SUCCESS POWER OF LOVE
HEALS MARRIAGE PROBLEMS

Many people are discovering this power in all departments of life. In the realm of human relationships it is all-powerful. A housewife told of having quarreled with her husband, after which he stormed out of the house. Since she had learned that she could generate love from within outward, she decided to try it in this marital crisis. Quietly she began to say over and over: "I CALL ON DIVINE LOVE TO HEAL OUR MARRIAGE NOW. I CALL ON DIVINE LOVE TO STRAIGHTEN OUT AND ADJUST THIS SITUATION."

In a little while, a sense of peace overwhelmed her, and she busily began preparing dinner for her husband in the faith that he would return to enjoy it. (After previous quarrels, it had not always been so.) Soon she heard the door open, and her husband entered, in a happy frame of mind, carrying a box of candy for her. Their quarrels became fewer and less severe, and in due time the disharmony in their marriage was entirely healed.

A businesswoman related a similar experience concerning the power of love in her marriage, which had been unhappy for some time. There had been many quarrels—much bickering, tension, disharmony. One night when there had been a prolonged and bitter quarrel, the woman thought: "We cannot go on. This disharmony is affecting our health, our business success, and our marriage. There must be a way out."

She began looking for something to read that might give her a sense of peace and hope, and she found these words: "LOVE MELTS SITUATIONS THAT SEEM IMPOSSIBLE." Over and over she said: "YES, IT IS TRUE. LOVE MELTS SITUATIONS THAT SEEM IMPOSSIBLE."

Formerly, reconciliation had come slowly and painstakingly after each quarrel. But as she continued dwelling on this statement of love, the disharmony and misunderstanding faded almost at once. That proved to be this couple's last bitter quarrel. Since that time, whenever the disharmony appeared, she has quickly affirmed, "LOVE MELTS SITUATIONS THAT SEEM IMPOSSIBLE." Always this has cleared the air and harmony has been reestablished.

THE AUTHOR'S EXPERIENCES
WITH LOVE IN FAMILY MATTERS

Do you doubt that your thoughts and words of divine love can have equivalent power in your own life and affairs? I once had a simple family experience that convinced me that our thoughts of love do reach others more quickly and completely than we sometimes realize. One warm spring day, I was in my study trying to finish an article on love when my teenage son came in. He had been playing golf all day and was hungry and anxious to get home to have some time with me.

When I explained that I was trying to complete an article and would finish in a few minutes, he silently left. Soon I thought I heard the study door open again, but since things at once became quiet, I did not turn to investigate. Some minutes later, when I completed my work, I realized that my son had returned noiselessly and placed two red roses from the nearby rose garden on my desk. Without a word he had then left, to wait patiently for me. He had not known I was working on an article on love. Never before had he brought me flowers, but at that moment he seemed attuned to the very ideas I was dwelling on in the article, and he lovingly responded.

On still another occasion, he demonstrated to me the success power of love. One morning he left for school in an unhappy mood. All day I remembered it and felt bad that he had begun the day in such a state of mind. I was certain there was something I should have done or said to turn the tide of his thinking in the morning. All day as I remembered this incident I kept affirming, "DIVINE LOVE IS DOING ITS PERFECT WORK IN THIS SITUATION NOW."

That afternoon when he arrived home from school, he came into the house, put aside his books, and greeted me with the words, "Hi, beautiful!" I cannot remember when he had greeted me in such a manner before, but truly, love had done its perfect work that day!

THE MISSION OF LOVE

When you are inclined to wonder how thoughts and words of love can do much good in resolving various problems, remind yourself that *loving words and loving thoughts seem supercharged with power to produce good.* Indeed, it is the mission of love, both personally and impersonally, to produce eternal good in your life. Your part is not to wonder how love works, but just to dare to begin releasing it from *within* yourself. When you do, you will always witness interesting and satisfying results.

LOVE CAN PROMOTE HEALTH

A doctor once showed me a medical book on psychosomatic illness. In this book, a group of physicians had compiled their analyses of various illnesses and of the mental and emotional attitudes they felt caused these illnesses. I was amazed to see that in every analysis, the need for love was listed.

For instance, in the case of stomach disorders of all types, one of the psychosomatic reasons given for such illness was "love needed." In the case of heart disorders, one of the reasons listed was "love needed."

In the case of skin disorders, one of the reasons listed was "need for approval," which is a form of love. (A bookkeeper stated that while experiencing a skin disorder on her face, she began a daily practice of placing her hands on her face and affirming, "DIVINE LOVE IS HEALING ME NOW," and the skin disorder soon faded.)

In the case of female disorders, one of the reasons listed was "need for love." In the case of chronic fatigue, one of the psychosomatic reasons listed was "depression, insecurity, and need for love."

In the case of both the common headache and migraine, one of the reasons listed was "insecurity and need for love." In the case of excessive weight and overeating, one of the reasons listed was "a feeling of dissatisfaction with life and a need for love." In the case of alcoholism and other excesses, one of the reasons listed was "feelings of inferiority and need for love."

The wonderful thing to remember is that when there is a need for love, we can begin supplying it from *within* ourselves. A businessman told me that he was healed of a painful condition of long standing after he began releasing love from within himself by speaking words of love to his body. He had tried various treatments to no avail. When he heard of the healing power of love, he began placing his hand on the painful area of his body and saying over and over, "I LOVE YOU." The pain subsided and gradually faded away.

Cancer has been described as an "anxiety disease." The emotional histories of a large percentage of those who have cancer show that in some period of their lives they felt anxious, insecure, or unloved, and that they subconsciously retained that feeling, which had often turned to bitterness and a critical state of mind, and may have even generated hostility and hate.

One authority has stated that sixty-two percent of his cancer patients told stories of loss, intense grief, depression, and despair that led up to their physical condition. As long ago as 1925, an analyst declared that after studying hundreds of cancer patients, she found most of them had suffered some difficult emotional crisis prior to the development of the disease, and that they had been unable to find effective outlets for their deep feelings and suppressed emotions.

LOVE HEALS
AN EMPLOYER'S UNPLEASANTNESS

In the field of prosperity, love as impersonal goodwill is all-powerful, too. It has been estimated that only fifteen percent of people's financial success is due to their technical ability, while eighty-five percent is due to their ability to get along with others. Some personnel managers believe that more than two-thirds of the people who lose their jobs do so not because of incompetence, but because they cannot get along with coworkers, clients, and customers. Other personnel managers have suggested that only about ten percent are discharged because of inadequate training or a lack of needed skills, whereas the other ninety percent are fired because of "personality problems."

A secretary once realized that in order to keep her job, which was interesting and well-paying, she would have to learn how to cope with her employer's unpleasant "morning disposition." She learned of the success power of love and began using one of Emmet Fox's statements: "ALL PEOPLE ARE EXPRESSIONS OF DIVINE LOVE; THEREFORE, I CAN MEET WITH NOTHING BUT THE EXPRESSIONS OF DIVINE LOVE."[*]

Beginning her day with this statement helped establish a peaceful atmosphere in the office for her employer's arrival. When he finally called her in for dictation, divine love had done its perfect work on his disposition. In time, his morning grouchiness and

---

[*] From "Treatment for Divine Love" (card), by Emmet Fox (DeVorss Publications, P.O. Box 1389, Camarillo, CA 93011-1389).

moodiness were replaced with a consistently pleasant attitude. The secretary felt her work in this regard was highly worthwhile, since the disposition of her boss had been the only unfavorable and worrisome aspect of her job.

LOVE PROSPERS A SALESMAN

Financially, an attitude of love is worthwhile, too. A traveling salesman who was heavily in debt attempted to get a loan from a bank to pay off his debts. Because he lacked collateral, he was not able to get the loan. He began to affirm, "DIVINE LOVE PROSPERS ME NOW." Within a few days he made a large sale and was able to pay off all his debts, with money left over.

HOW LOVE BROUGHT PROSPERITY
IN THE MIDST OF A RECESSION

A number of years ago during a financial recession, and in bitter cold weather, the company for which I was working experienced financial difficulties. Members of the board of directors had become depressed because of the weather, which seemed to be delaying the company's prosperity. They were also depressed about general economic conditions. It appeared to be a hopeless situation until several persons working for the company agreed to begin affirming together, at specific times, statements on the prospering power of love. The individuals each affirmed for themselves and their own inspiration: "I AM THE LOVE OF GOD IN EXPRESSION. I LET GOD'S LOVE

GUIDE, DIRECT, AND INSPIRE ME." The statement they used for the company's prosperity was: "GOD'S LOVE IN US IS DRAWING TO US NEW IDEAS, NEW COURAGE, AND VISIBLE DAILY SUPPLY."

The atmosphere of depression and hopelessness concerning the business situation seemed to lift. Continued use of the prayers caused all those involved to experience an uplifted state of mind. New ideas and new courage attracted visible daily supply. Within a few weeks the financial crisis had passed, and that year proved to be one of the most prosperous the company had ever known!

A chiropractor who was having similar financial challenges asked how this firm managed to make a financial comeback in the midst of bad weather and an economic recession. Those prayers were shared with him, and his financial results were so satisfying that he obtained a thousand printed copies of the prayers, which he distributed to his patients whenever they mentioned their own financial challenges. Thus the power of love proved its prospering power to many people that winter in our area.

HOW TO SUCCEED THROUGH LOVE

Many years ago, Emma Curtis Hopkins gave some financial advice along this line when she wrote, "Take your business as it is, and praise divine love that there is a strong, wise way out of your dilemma." So when there is such a need, affirm, "I PRAISE DIVINE LOVE THAT THERE IS A STRONG, WISE WAY OUT OF THIS DILEMMA."

In all phases of life, love is a success power. Many people who are seeking a balanced life have found this prayer helpful: "DIVINE LOVE, EXPRESSING THROUGH ME, NOW DRAWS TO ME ALL THAT IS NEEDED TO MAKE ME HAPPY AND TO MAKE MY LIFE COMPLETE."

Whatever your need in life may be, love is the answer. You do not have to look outside yourself for love. Begin releasing it from within your own thoughts and feelings, and you will attract to you whatever people, situations, and conditions are for your highest good. Truly, "YOU WALK IN THE CHARMED CIRCLE OF GOD'S LOVE, AND YOU ARE DIVINELY IRRESISTIBLE TO YOUR HIGHEST GOOD NOW." This is the prospering power of love.

LOVE YOUR WAY
TO SUCCESS

— Chapter 2 —

How often we try to battle our way through life, experiencing disappointment, pain, and failure at every turn, when we could much more easily love our way through life, experiencing success every step of the way!

Emmet Fox once wrote, "There is no difficulty that enough love will not conquer."*

I recall once having a problem that (I thought) I had tried in every way to solve. Still it was as though I faced a stone wall.

Other persons from a particular firm were involved. Until they took action, I was helpless to do anything more, I reasoned. It seemed a particularly frustrating situation, since they would not give attention to the requests I made. I had prodded these per-

---

* From "Love" (card), by Emmet Fox (DeVorss Publications, P.O. Box 1389, Camarillo, CA 93011-1389).

sons in every way I knew and still they had not taken action. It seemed hopeless, until one day I read these words by Emma Curtis Hopkins:[*]

> Everything is really full of love for you . . . The good that is for you loves you as much as you love it. The good that is for you seeks you and will come flying to you if you see that what you love is love itself. All people will change when you know that they are love. We shall change toward all people when we know that we ourselves are formed out of love. All is love. There is nothing in all the universe but love.

When I read those words, it was as though something hard broke up inside of me. I actually felt something hard move in the area of my heart; then it seemed to dissolve and I was able to breathe more freely.

Truly, there had been a stone wall in this situation, just as I had sensed. But that stone wall had not been an outer physical structure towering over me. The stone wall was actually within me, in the form of my own hard thoughts about the situation. It was a revelation, a surprise, and finally a relief to realize that not someone else, but my own hard thinking had been the barrier that caused the situation to remain at a standstill.

---

[*] From *Scientific Christian Mental Practice* by Emma Curtis Hopkins (DeVorss Publications, P.O. Box 1389, Camarillo, CA 93011-1389).

I began to affirm: "EVERYTHING IS REALLY FULL OF LOVE FOR ME, INCLUDING THOSE PERSONS. THE GOOD THAT IS FOR ME IN THIS SITUATION LOVES ME AS MUCH AS I LOVE IT. THE GOOD THAT IS FOR ME IN THIS MATTER NOW SEEKS ME AND COMES FLYING TO ME AS I BEHOLD THIS SITUATION WITH LOVE."

Within a few days I heard from the persons involved, though I had not heard from them previously for many months. Their letter seemed especially cordial, and it stated that they were immediately expediting the matter in which I was interested. Now, whenever I have any business contact with this firm, they always respond graciously and speedily. Never since that time has there been any delay or misunderstanding.

You can love your way through any troublesome situation by declaring: "THIS PERSON AND THIS SITUATION ARE REALLY FULL OF LOVE FOR ME, AND I AM FULL OF LOVE FOR THEM. I PRAISE DIVINE LOVE IN THIS MATTER NOW. I BEHOLD THIS SITUATION WITH LOVE."

THE AUTHOR'S USE OF LOVE AS A SECRET WEAPON FOR SUCCESS

Some years ago I had another experience that proved to me that there is nothing weak about love; that love can win more battles than fists or instruments of destruction; that love is our "secret weapon" for successful results.

I was asked to take a job as director of a nonprofit organization. It was a job that no one else wanted because there had been great disharmony in this organi-

zation. Along with the ill feeling that had been generated, financial lack had also appeared. It was not a job
to look forward to, especially since this would be my
first assignment after entering a new field of work. I
had proper training for the job, but no experience.
This hardly seemed a suitable assignment for an inexperienced person, but it was this job or none for the
present, so I reluctantly took it.

At my first meeting with the board of directors of
the organization, things did not look promising. Two
of the directors objected to my job appointment, saying I was too young and inexperienced to straighten
things out. Silently, I agreed with them wholeheartedly. But the other board members pointed out that I
was the new director, having been trained and assigned to this job by the home office, and that they
planned to work with me to straighten out any difficulties in whatever way I felt was best.

As I prayed for guidance about this challenging
job, the thought came to me that divine love was to be
my secret weapon; that love could win in this situation and could bring victorious results, harmony, and
prosperity to this organization.

When I expressed these thoughts at that first board
meeting, my ideas on divine love only provoked the
two objecting board members, who scoffed at using
the "mere" power of love for solving anything. They
"told me off" for even suggesting such a thing and
then they resigned. This proved to be love's first step
in clearing away disharmony.

In private conversation, the chairman of the board
of directors agreed with me that there was nothing
weak about divine love; that divine love could win

this battle. He believed so strongly in the harmonizing, prospering power of love to make things right that he agreed to meet with me for an hour every morning so we might discuss the various affairs of the organization and affirm the perfect results of divine love.

The affirmations we used in those daily morning meetings were: "DIVINE LOVE IS DOING ITS PERFECT WORK HERE AND NOW. DIVINE LOVE HARMONIZES, DIVINE LOVE ADJUSTS, DIVINE LOVE PROSPERS. DIVINE LOVE FORESEES EVERYTHING AND RICHLY PROVIDES EVERY GOOD THING FOR THIS ORGANIZATION NOW. DIVINE LOVE IS NOW VICTORIOUS!"

The results of those daily meetings were almost unbelievable. As we poured forth words of divine love into this troubled situation, it was like pouring out a healing balm. Attitudes and actions became quiet, peaceful, harmonious, cooperative. Soon it seemed as though there had never been any difficulty in the organization. Peace and harmony reigned in all its activities.

As we continued daily affirmations of divine love, new people, new activity, new prosperity flowed into this organization. The financial income soon doubled. A number of gifts came, including fresh paint and willing painters who applied it to the building free of charge. New drapes, lovely new furnishings, air conditioners, a public-address system, and other needed kinds of equipment were provided. The entire building that housed the organization was beautifully redecorated within a few months.

The organization went on to new growth, new progress, new prosperity. Soon no one spoke of or cared about the former trouble, since everything was so wonderful in the present. Though I am no longer connected with that organization, it has continued to grow and prosper over the years. Divine love met and solved my challenges there; divine love has continued to do its perfect work in that group.

THE PROBLEM-SOLVING
POWER OF LOVE

A housewife decided to use love as her secret weapon in a troublesome situation. For months she had been speaking of her "no-good" husband. He was a miner who left home every spring to find work in the gold and silver mines of the Northwest. Usually after he left for the mines, she did not hear from him again until late fall, when he came home to loaf all winter.

During the summer months, she was left at home alone to work as a waitress or to do anything else she could to feed and clothe herself and pay the bills. She had been contemplating divorce because life with her husband seemed a hopeless struggle for existence.

It was then that she learned of the problem-solving power of love. Instead of continuing to dwell upon her husband's faults, she began to decree that divine love was doing its perfect work in her marriage, in their financial affairs, and in her husband's job prospects. Good things began to happen.

Her husband wrote her that he had obtained work in a silver mine and that he would begin sending money home regularly after he received his first pay-check. Since he had never previously sent money home, this seemed a miracle. Though in the past he had not written at all when he was away, he now wrote long, friendly letters regularly, even speaking of his desire for himself and his wife to have a good life together.

At the end of the summer mining season, he wrote that he had work for the winter, too. This was unusual since his type of work had always been seasonal. As his wife continued to affirm the perfect outworking of divine love, he finally returned home, was able to re-pay their long-standing debts, and their marriage be-came completely harmonized. Her husband formed his own mining corporation and went into business for himself. He helped her start her own business, which she manages while he is away in the mines. It is a business they work in together when he is not otherwise occupied.

How often people have missed the blessings and security of a happy marriage and a good life because they have condemned and criticized rather than loved their way through the challenges that confronted them! Yet how much easier it is to love your way through a problem than to battle your way through it!

CRITICISM CAN BRING
NEGATIVE RESULTS

The unloving, unnecessary results that people of-ten bring on themselves through criticism (the oppo-site of love) recall the story of the young artist who had a genius (he thought) for picking out the faults and weaknesses of other people. He prided himself on seeing the unworthy traits in their character. One night this young man had a dream in which he saw himself walking on a barren road, struggling wearily beneath a heavy burden.

In the dream he cried out weakly, "What is this heavy weight I have to carry? Why must I carry it? Why should I be so burdened?"

A voice answered: "Your burden is the weight of all the faults you have found in other people. Why do you complain? You discovered those faults. Should they not, therefore, belong to you?"

The description of evil doubles the appearance of evil. *Whatever form of evil you see in others, you are inviting into your own life as some form of negation.* When you "run down" someone else with your criticism and condemnation, you are opening the way for your own mind, body, or affairs to become "run down" with ill health, unhappiness, confusion, or financial lack.

A group of employees quit their jobs at a business firm because they did not like the new manager. They continued to belittle and condemn the new manager after they were no longer connected with the firm. As they continued in their negative judgments, one of these former employees had a heart attack and died within a few months. Another former employee opened a new business; it soon failed. Later he opened several other businesses, and they failed. He also became estranged from several members of his family.

Other former employees of the firm who remained critical had similar destructive experiences. One businesswoman had a stroke, developed paralysis, and passed on within a year, though she previously had enjoyed many healthy years of active living. Another person developed arthritis and soon could walk only on crutches. Still another person had several bouts of pneumonia and had to be hospitalized frequently. The physical suffering of these people was also attended by heavy financial expense and by other business problems. *The unjust criticisms these people had meant for someone else hurt only themselves.*

As for the new manager, he was aware of the backstairs gossip but ignored it, for he knew it had no power. Both he and his business prospered.

HOW TO HANDLE
YOUR INITIATIONS IN LOVE

The ancients knew another success secret we should know: the description of good doubles good! May Rowland, in her book *Dare to Believe!*, has written about how you can double the good in your life:

> If you are not attracting the good that you desire in your life, learn to express love; become a radiating center of love; and you will find that love, the divine magnet within you, will change your whole world. . . . When your heart is filled with love you

will not be critical or irritable, but you will be divinely irresistible.[*]

Florence Scovel Shinn wrote, "Every man on this planet is taking his initiation in love."[†] *Whatever your problem, it is but a test in love. If you meet that test through love, your problem will be solved. If you do not meet that test through love, your problem will continue until you do! Your problem is your initiation in love.*

A businesswoman recently related how she met her initiation in love:

> Only a short time ago, I felt I could not go on. My husband was on the brink of a nervous breakdown and in deep depression. Our oldest son, age nineteen, was struggling to stay in college, doing it all on his own, without a dime of help from us. Our middle son, age twelve, had been under treatment for several years as an emotionally disturbed child. He has periods of becoming quite angry, on the edge of violence. Our daughter, age eleven, was beginning to react to all this discord with temper tantrums and sulking spells, and seemed unable to get

---

[*] *Dare to Believe*, by May Rowland (Unity School of Christianity, Unity Village, MO 64065, 1961).

[†] *The Game of Life and How to Play It,* by Florence Scovel Shinn (DeVorss Publications, P.O. Box 1389, Camarillo, CA 93011-1389, 1925).

along harmoniously with her friends or teachers. I kept getting one kidney infection after another. Since I have only one kidney, you can understand the concern I felt when my doctor warned me to be especially careful.

After reading an article about the power of divine love to improve personalities, situations, events, even one's health, I bought a notebook and a pen. Every time I started to worry, feel sick or afraid, I sat down, relaxed, wrote the name of the family member or the situation that was bothering me, and then I wrote down a decree of love about it. For my husband, our children, and for myself, I often wrote over and over: "I BEHOLD YOU WITH THE EYES OF LOVE AND I GLORY IN YOUR PERFECTION."

The results were almost unbelievable! My husband was at a standstill when I began using the power of love on our affairs six weeks ago. Recently he took a bath, the first in weeks; he got his hair cut and turned out some work on his own, without a word of prodding from me. Our son in college received a one-hundred-dollar refund on income tax. He also got a job managing the baseball team, so his tuition will be provided. Our middle son has gone for several weeks now without displaying violent behavior. His disposition has greatly improved. Our daughter is getting along better with her friends and teachers. As for my kidney infection, it has cleared up completely, and I am now launching a health program to build up my resistance. I have also obtained a part-time job. You can see why I shall always be grateful that I learned about the problem-solving power of love!

CALL FORTH LOVE
TO OVERCOME ALL DIFFICULTIES

Charles Fillmore has written:

The more we talk about love, the stronger it grows in consciousness, and if we persist in thinking loving thoughts and speaking loving words, we are sure to bring into our experience the feeling of that great love that is beyond description—the very love of God. . . . You may trust love to get you out of your difficulties. There is nothing too hard for it to accomplish for you, if you put your confidence in it.*

Love works in varied ways to produce right results—when it is recognized and called forth in a situation. As you begin to think more about how you can love *your* way through life, rather than about how you have to battle *your* way through life, love will reveal to you its secret success powers. Launch forth on the great venture of love and affirm often along the

---

* *Talks on Truth,* by Charles Fillmore (Unity School of Christianity, Unity Village, MO 64065, 1926).

way: "I LIVE BY THE LAW OF LOVE, AND LOVE IS NOW VICTORIOUS." This one thought can win many a battle in your life.

LOVE ACTIVATES
A HEALING POWER

— Chapter 3 —

During the spring season, various religious groups observe periods of prayer and fasting, which symbolize a time of preparation for the resurrection of new life and beauty in their personal world. In springtime and all through the year, let's stop crucifying and start resurrecting! We can do this through the healing power of love.

What you should do during your fasting is to abstain from recalling negative memories of the past — grudges, criticisms, spite, feelings of injustice and hurt, and other inharmonies. There are definite, simple ways you can pour out the healing power of love on your negative memories, so you can be free of them forever. As you become free of these destructive thoughts and feelings, you cease crucifying yourself and others, and you are then ready for resurrected good.

41

A businesswoman in France reported:

> My aunt is responding at last to the waves of divine love I have been radiating to her. She now refers to me as her "beloved niece." This was a very negative relationship that divine love has now reversed!

SPECIAL PHASES OF LOVE:
FORGIVENESS AND RELEASE

There are two special ways you can fast from negative attitudes and tune in on the healing power of love, which makes you whole in mind, body, and affairs. These special ways are the act of *release* and the act of *forgiveness*. Perhaps it surprises you to hear that release and forgiveness are parts of love. Yet *when you find that other phases of love have not healed some troublesome condition in your life, you may discover that it is because you have not invoked the releasing, forgiving phases of love*. When you do, satisfying results will surely come.

Kahlil Gibran might have been describing these two important phases of love when he wrote: "Speak to us of love. . . . Even as he [love] is for your growth so is he for your pruning . . . think not you can direct the course of love, for love, if it finds you worthy, directs your course."*

---

* Reprinted from *The Prophet,* by Kahlil Gibran, with permission of the publisher, Alfred A. Knopf, Inc. Copyright 1923 by Kahlil

You have heard it said that love is a many-splendored thing, but often when the pruning power of love is at work in your life, you may feel that love is a "many-splintered" thing. And yet, when you are willing to release and forgive, the splinter (or "thorn in the flesh") is transformed into a splendid result, and you find that love is able to direct your course to greater good.

Through release and forgiveness you break up, cross out, and dissolve—and you are freed forever from—the negative attitudes and memories that have limited you to less than the highest and best in your life experience.

The freeing, forgiving attitude likewise "raises" your good and brings it to life. Invoke the healing power of love through freeing and forgiving the negative experiences of your past and present, and you will find yourself well on the way to resurrected good.

Many people consider *forgive* an unpleasant word, but it means simply to set free, to liberate, by "giving" something positive in place of, or "for," something negative. *It is spiritual law that you must forgive if you want to overcome your own difficulties and make any real progress in life.*

RELEASE IS A FORM OF FORGIVENESS

Release is a form of forgiveness that we all need to practice often. Although we usually think of emo-

---

Gibran; renewal copyright 1951 by Administrators C.T.A. of Kahlil Gibran estate, and Mary G. Gibran.

tional attachment as one of the highest forms of love, quite the opposite is true. Emotional *release* is one of the highest forms of love. Attachment leads to bondage, whereas the way of true love is to *free* that which you love. *You never lose anything through release. Instead, you open the way for a freer, more satisfying type of love to develop, where everyone involved is able to give and receive love in a more harmonious way.*

You never lose that which is for your highest good, under any circumstances. When it seems that you have lost something, it is because it is no longer best for you. Though you may feel that it *is* still best, you have actually outgrown it, and the pruning power of love has released you from it. Realizing this, you are able to free it and open your mind and heart to receive your new and higher good.

Setting others free means setting yourself free. When you feel bound to other people—their attitudes, their behavior, their way of life—it is because you are (perhaps unconsciously) binding *them* to *you*. Then you begin to feel constricted, chafing against the very bondage you have caused! Always, you yourself hold the key to your freedom from bondage. You turn the key to that freedom when you release the personality, problem, or condition you think is clutching you. Remember, you are the master, never the slave, of circumstances.

You become victor instead of victim when you dare to speak the word of release to the person or thing you think is binding you. You are your own bondage made manifest. You can become your own release made manifest, too.

A businesswoman in Florida wrote:

I was especially interested to read in *The Pros-pering Power of Love* that when you are in a situa-tion where you are being dominated, it is because *you* have formed a "binding action" and you need to "forgive and release."

After I read this, and daily practiced release, a disharmonious work situation became friendly and comfortable. Releasing, forgiving, and loving: these prayer methods have blessed me beyond all my ex-pectations!

THE HEALING POWER OF RELEASE

A housewife had worried for many months over her husband's illness. The more she tried to help him recover, the more he seemed to cling to his illness and the more confined they both were. One day she learned of the healing power of release and began to declare for her husband: "I RELEASE YOU NOW TO YOUR HIGHEST GOOD. I LOVE YOU BUT I RELEASE YOU TO COMPLETE FREEDOM AND COMPLETE HEALTH IN WHATEVER WAY IS BEST. I AM FREE AND YOU ARE FREE."

When this woman had previously tried to help her husband by using various healing affirmations, he had seemed subconsciously to resist her attempts to will him to health. After she began to release him to find health in his own way, ceased any mental effort in his direction, and began to lead a more normal life her-self, her husband's health rapidly improved. Some of his ailments disappeared completely. He experienced the healing power of love as it worked through release.

Most human-relations problems would melt away if people would practice the healing power of release, instead of trying to make others over in a certain image or trying to force them to do things in a certain way.

Nowhere is there more need for the expression of love as release than between husbands and wives, between parents and children. We often try to bend others to our will, calling it love when it is really selfish possessiveness—that binds instead of frees. Then we wonder why others resist instead of accepting our "help."

Gibran described the loving attitude of release in marriage: "Love one another, but make not a bond of love . . . let there be spaces in your togetherness. . . . Sing and dance together and be joyous, but let each one of you be alone . . . stand together yet not too near together."[*]

He described the loving attitude of release toward children in these words: "Your children are not your children. They are the sons and daughters of Life's longing for itself. They come through you but not from you, and though they are with you yet they belong not to you. . . . You may house their bodies but not their souls. . . . You may strive to be like them, but seek not to make them like you."[†]

---

[*] Gibran, *The Prophet.*

[†] Gibran, *The Prophet.*

A MOTHER-DAUGHTER RELATIONSHIP
HEALED THROUGH RELEASE

A counselor was once called to a hospital to visit a young woman who had experienced a nervous breakdown. She was having severe headaches and prolonged crying spells. Drugs and medication had brought no relief.

Her mother was frantic with fear, saying: "I can't understand what has happened. This girl has always been such an obedient child. She has never disagreed with me, nor crossed me in any way. But now she is saying terrible things to me. She tells me I've ruined her life, that I have kept her from getting a job and working; that I've kept her from marrying and having a normal life. To be sure, I never encouraged her to work, because she had always been a timid, sickly child. There was no financial reason for her to work, and so I insisted that she remain at home and help out there, thinking it would provide her with a more pleasant way of life. Now she is criticizing and condemning me for it. She suddenly seems to hate me."

Her daughter, who was finally rebelling against her mother's domination and "smother love," was hardly a child. She was past thirty, though she still wore bobby socks, long hair, and teenage clothes. She also seemed to think and talk like a teenager.

The daughter felt quite guilty about having turned against her mother, but she said she could not help it. When assured by the counselor that she was reacting in a normal way, she began to relax. As she did, the severe headaches left her completely. Her crying ceased. She was able to retain food again, and her

strength returned. Much of the hostility toward her
mother soon faded away.

In further talks with this mother and daughter, the
counselor helped them both to realize that this experience had been for the good. Had this daughter not
been able to release her accumulated hostilities toward her mother, had she not been able to begin
claiming her emotional independence, she would
doubtless have faced years of continued unhappiness
as well as the need for extensive therapy. The statis-
tics of mental illness show that most of it arises from
disharmonious relationships in the home — relationships that are usually possessive and dominating.
Mental illness is the patient's way of fighting that
domination and escaping from possessiveness.

Your dear ones must have liberty to live their own
lives, and you must grant it to them, or else you will
create problems for them and for yourself. *If you want
to free yourself from all types of problems in mind,
body, and affairs, you must release others to find
their good in their own way.* A clear channel is then
opened for a great good to come to all involved. Your
own freedom and well-being depend upon such release, as do the freedom and well-being of your loved
ones.

RELEASE FREES A MOTHER AND SON

A professional woman was quite concerned about
her bachelor son. He was very successful in his work
but had never married, and still lived with his mother.
A widow, she devoted many years of her life to rear-
ing and educating this son. Now the time had come

when she wished to be free to travel and perhaps to work elsewhere. She also longed to see her son happily married. She realized that her own freedom and well-being depended upon her releasing her son emotionally.

Then it seemed that her dreams were coming true: her son met the girl of his choice. But instead of being happy about it, his mother became upset and resentful, constantly finding fault with the girl. Soon the mother became ill, and her physician told her she was suffering from hypertension caused by some secret anxiety.

She then realized that in order to be free from illness, in order to live a happy, balanced life, she must free her son to live his life as he wished. She realized that setting him free meant setting herself free. For this purpose she constantly affirmed: "I FULLY AND FREELY RELEASE YOU. I LOOSE YOU AND LET YOU GO TO YOUR GOOD. THE GOOD OF ONE IS THE GOOD OF ALL." Before long, all anxiety left her, her health improved, and her son was married. This left her free to travel, to seek new work, and to develop the whole new, freer way of life she had long wanted.

When your prayers have not been answered, it is often because you need to practice release—release of some person or situation, some financial difficulty or health problem. Often it is not an enemy you need to release but a friend, a relative—a husband, wife, or child. As you practice release, your problem is solved, your good is resurrected.

YOU MUST FORGIVE
FOR YOUR OWN SAKE

Forgiveness is a very important type of release, and a most important form of love. When you practice forgiveness, you experience the healing power of love. You must forgive injuries and hurts of the past and present—not so much for the other person's sake as for your own. Resentment, condemnation, anger, and the desire to "get even" or to see someone punished or hurt are things that rot your soul. They bind you to many other problems that actually have nothing to do with the original grievances.

Emmet Fox has explained:

> When you hold resentment against anyone, you are bound to that person by a cosmic link, a real though mental chain. You are tied by a cosmic tie to the thing that you hate. The one person perhaps in the whole world whom you most dislike is the very one to whom you are attaching yourself by a hook that is stronger than steel.[*]

A HOUSEWIFE'S FORGIVENESS
BRINGS HEALING AND PROSPERITY

A housewife recently described how the healing power of love worked in her family through forgiveness: "Ten months ago my whole world seemed to have crashed to pieces. My husband's job, managerial

---

[*] *The Sermon on the Mount*, by Emmet Fox (Harper & Row, New York, 1938).

in nature, was suddenly (and apparently unfairly) terminated. Two of our children and I were very sick with bronchial infections. I also had a recurrence of a bladder infection. It was at this hopeless point in our affairs that I was introduced to one of the Ponder prosperity books, which I began to study. In it I read something I needed very much: 'I FULLY AND FREELY FORGIVE. I LOOSE AND LET GO. I CAST ALL JUDGMENTS, RESENTMENTS, CRITICISM, AND UNFORGIVENESS UPON THE CHRIST WITHIN, TO BE DISSOLVED AND HEALED. THE PROSPERING TRUTH HAS SET ME FREE TO MEET MY RICH GOOD AND TO SHARE MY GOOD WITH OTHERS!'

"As I read these words, I realized I had been openly resentful toward my husband's former employer because of his seeming unfairness and poor business judgment. I kept using the affirmations in the book and actually it became very easy to forgive completely.

"Within the next few days my infection was gone, a skin ailment of my mother's disappeared, and then our financial demonstrations began! Our debts had seemed insurmountable; but gradually, through a complete change of mind brought about by forgiveness, money began to come from unexpected sources. We received an income tax refund; my parents sent money to cover the rent; our creditors did not press us for money. After being unemployed for two months, my husband was led to the right job, one which he thoroughly understands, as general manager of a ski resort which is under construction now and which we will move to shortly. The corporation is building us a wonderful apartment, fully carpeted and decorated to our taste."

When we hold resentment toward another, we are bound to that person or condition by a cosmic link, and forgiveness is the only way to dissolve that link and be free.

WHAT IT MEANS WHEN OTHERS
HURT OR DISAPPOINT YOU

Since other persons are children of God, there is really nothing to forgive. They have not really failed us, or disappointed us, or let us down, or shamed us. They may have stumbled while crossing our pathway. But they were children of God who had temporarily lost their way. If they crossed our pathway, it was because they needed and wanted our blessing. They were unconsciously looking to us so they could be steadied and set right.

Our progress has not been hindered, no matter what they did or did not do. They did not, they could not, keep our good from us. They crossed our path by divine appointment, even though they seemed to hurt us for a little while. *When people bother us in any way, it is because their souls are trying to get our divine attention, and our blessing. When we give them that, they no longer bother us. They fade out of our lives and find their good elsewhere.*

A nurse found great comfort and truth in these words after she was seriously injured in a collision with a car driven by an intoxicated man. After recovering, she returned to her nursing profession. Again and again the man responsible for the collision was admitted to the hospital where she worked—and always he was in an intoxicated state. She refused to nurse him, and was assured by his doctor that she would not be assigned to his case.

Once when he was admitted, there was a shortage of nurses on her floor, and she was the only nurse available when the nurse-call light came on in his room. Since it was unavoidable, she took him his tray and medicine. When she appeared, he recognized her, talked about the accident, and told her he had been worried about her financial affairs after the accident, realizing that she was widowed with children to care for.

In the wee hours of the morning, as they talked, he asked her forgiveness, and she gave it. The amazing thing was that following their conversation, he gradually stopped drinking, and she never heard of his being admitted to the hospital again. She realized that the man seemed to have wanted her forgiveness and blessing. When he got that, he faded out of her life.

HOW A LUMP WAS HEALED

If you do not know what or who you need to forgive when your good seems withheld from you, ask God to reveal to you what or whom you need to forgive. You may be surprised to find where the block is!

A woman discovered a lump in her breast and was greatly frightened by it. But instead of rushing out to talk about it to anyone, she decided to analyze the situation mentally and pray for guidance.

She realized that a hard condition in the body symbolizes a hard condition in the mind -hard thoughts of resentment, condemnation, unforgiveness. She prayed, "Divine Intelligence, what or whom do I need to forgive?"

Since the answer did not come immediately, she continued every day to pray, meditate, and ask: "Divine Intelligence, what or whom do I need to forgive? What hard attitudes do I need to release, give up, in order to be forgiven of this condition?" In meditation one day she found herself thinking about her husband and a woman with whom he had been involved five years previously. At the time, she had met the experience nonresistantly, and it had faded away. She and her husband were now happier than ever, but she realized in this meditation period that she still had hard thoughts toward the other woman and toward her husband concerning the distressing experiences during that period.

She prayed for the other woman, blessed her, and released her, saying to her mentally: "I FREELY FORGIVE YOU. I LET YOU GO. YOU HAVE GONE TO MEET YOUR GOOD AND TO SHARE YOUR GOOD ELSEWHERE. IT IS DONE, IT IS FINISHED." To her husband she mentally said: "I FREELY FORGIVE YOU. I LET GO ALL FALSE CONCEPTS ABOUT YOU. YOU ARE A FAITHFUL, LOVING HUSBAND, AND WE HAVE A WONDERFUL MARRIAGE. ONLY GOOD HAS COME FROM THAT EXPERIENCE."

She declared these words of forgiveness in her prayer time for several weeks. One day she realized that the lump in her breast was gone; she never knew when it disappeared.

A SURE REMEDY FOR RESURRECTING
HEALTH, WEALTH, AND HAPPINESS

Deliberately practice the healing power of love through acts of forgiveness and release. Charles Fillmore describes this as a "sure remedy" for resurrecting health, wealth, and happiness:

> Bless your problem, whatever it be, with a thought somewhat like this: "I NOW RELEASE YOU AND BLESS YOU. DIVINE LOVE IS ADJUSTING MY LIFE AND ITS PROBLEMS. REALIZING THIS, I ABIDE IN PEACE.". . . Every person who thus allies himself with the power of divine love creates a bit of heaven on earth.

A schoolteacher in Oklahoma confirmed this when she wrote:

> I have given my niece a copy of *The Prospering Power of Love,* and she recently spent an entire afternoon telling me how that book has revolutionized her life.
>
> She and her husband of forty years had been having some serious marital difficulties. So she decided to work for a whole month on forgiveness, as outlined in the book.
>
> When her husband returned home from his traveling job at the end of that month, his entire attitude had changed. He told her how lovely she looked. He asked how she had managed to lose ten pounds, and

he said she appeared more relaxed. His pleasant attitudes seemed a miracle.

THE RESURRECTING
POWER OF LOVE

Chapter 4

The word *resurrect* means "to bring to view again . . . to restore to life." The resurrection of Jesus Christ was for the purpose of bringing to view again the divine nature of all humanity.

Men and women were created with a divine nature, in the image of God. But they misused their divine nature by turning their attention to a belief in evil, and so they forgot about their divinity and how to use it.

Some of the great characters of the Old Testament tried to bring the divine nature of humanity back to notice, back into use. David sang of this divinity: "Yet thou hast made him little less than God, and dost crown him with glory and honor." (Psalm 8:5) "You are gods, sons of the Most High, all of you." (Psalm 82:6) Job realized, ". . . there is a spirit in man." (Job 32:8)

Spiritual humanity has always been crowned with glory and honor, though it lost sight of its glorious divinity for many centuries. In order to bring this divinity into view again, to restore it to life, a loving Father sent a Savior, a Redeemer—one who would resurrect an awareness of the divinity of all humanity.

YOU CAN BE FREED FROM
ALL KINDS OF LIMITATION

The raising up of the Christ nature in the man Jesus symbolizes the resurrection of the Christ nature in all humanity. Jesus described humanity's divinity when He said, "The kingdom of God is in the midst of you." (Luke 17:21) *What theology calls a "lost soul" is merely a soul that has lost sight of its divinity. When our divine nature is brought back into view, into use, it can lift us out of all kinds of limitation.*

A housewife from Pennsylvania wrote:

> I had a copy of *The Prospering Power of Love* in my pocketbook when I visited my daughter in the hospital. I noticed how depressed a young lady was in the next bed, so I offered her my book. She accepted it gladly, and here is the note she wrote me later:
>
> "I can't thank you enough for sharing with me *The Prospering Power of Love*. I am not a religious fanatic, but God has changed my life immensely since I began study of that book, and learned that I have a divine nature. If I had not been introduced to those ideas and used them, I would be in bad shape

today, both mentally and physically. Instead I am
well on the way to total recovery in every way."

A statement I have used many times over the
years, one that has helped lift me out of limitation, is
this: "CHRIST IN ME NOW FREES ME FROM ALL
LIMITATION. I AM THE RESURRECTION AND THE
LIFE."

Paul said that this resurrected Christ nature in individuals is the mystery that has been hidden for gen-
erations, and he described it as their hope of glory. He
reminded the early Christians of their divinity: "Do
you not know that your body is a temple of the Holy
Spirit within you, which you have from God? . . . So
glorify God in your body." (1 Corinthians 6:19, 20)

Charles Fillmore described resurrection as the
"raising up of the whole man—spirit, soul, and
body—into the Christ consciousness of life and
wholeness." He wrote in *Keep a True Lent:*

> The time is ripe for the advent of a new race, the
> advent of the spiritualized man. This will be
> brought about not by a miracle or the fiat of God,
> but by the gradual refinement of the man of the
> flesh into the man of Spirit. The true overcomer is
> qualifying himself to become a member of the new
> spiritualized race.*

---

* *Keep a True Lent,* by Charles Fillmore (Unity School of Christianity, Unity Village, MO 64065, 1953).

Just as Jesus, through His resurrection of His spiritual nature, brought back into notice this spiritualized individual, so we can bring alive the divinity within us and in other people. As we do, we become a part of the spiritualized race which overcomes, or "comes up over," the negative experiences of life.

"Think of yourself in a large way, and the little things of life will lose interest for you," says Charles Fillmore. "See all things from the large viewpoint. Instead of seeing yourself as mere man, see yourself as divine being. The only difference between gods and men is in comprehension. Men have the power to comprehend and appropriate all they have imagined possible with God."

HOW PRAISE CAN EXPAND YOUR GOOD

From a practical standpoint, you can see yourself and others in a large way, as divine beings, through praise. Praise is one of the strongest forms of love. Praise expands your good. Praise is your resurrecting power because it brings back into notice and use, back to life, the good in yourself and in others. Ella Wheeler Wilcox was expressing the highest form of praise in her poem "Attainment," when she wrote:

> *Know that you are great,*
> *Great with divinity.*

The word *praise* means to express approval, to glorify, to appraise as good. When you express approval of yourself or others, you are glorifying the divine in yourself and others. Always you can resurrect or bring back to notice the good, the divinity in people and situations through praise.

Say to yourself often: "THROUGH THE POWER OF CHRIST IN ME, MY LIFE CAN BE AS WONDERFUL AS I WANT IT TO BE!" Whether it seems literally true or not, begin to think of yourself as glorious, splendid, beloved, strong, well, capable. Begin to think of the world as a beautiful place in which to live, work, grow, play. Affirm often for others, especially those who trouble you: "THROUGH THE POWER OF CHRIST IN YOU, YOUR LIFE CAN BE AS WONDERFUL AS YOU WANT IT TO BE!" You will be surprised how this simple, delightful way of thinking will resurrect—bring back to notice, restore to life—your good. Also, declare often for any situation that troubles you: "I APPRAISE THIS SITUATION AS GOOD."

A BOOKKEEPER IMPROVED
HER EMPLOYER'S DISPOSITION

I once knew of an employer for whom no one liked to work. This solemn, serious man was irritable, impatient, hard to please. One bookkeeper who had worked for him for many years finally had to resign because of illness. Everyone wondered what would become of the employer, since nobody wanted the bookkeeper's job. None of the local townspeople applied for it.

Instead, an out-of-town bookkeeper took the job. She was a happy, jolly, attractive person, quite in contrast to the serious, drab, complaining woman who had previously worked for this man. She obviously expected to have a good time in her new job. She was appraising the situation as good.

She planned each day around her new employer's well-being. She came in early to beautify his office and set things in order before beginning the day. She often brought fresh flowers for his desk from her garden. She inquired about how he wanted everything done and made it a point to please him. She often complimented him on some aspect of his work, or perhaps on his wife and family, who came in the office frequently. By making things as pleasant as possible, the bookkeeper slowly transformed her employer into a calm, peaceful, happy individual.

For the first time in years, he smiled regularly and genuinely. It was a joy to those about him to observe him so happy and relaxed. In his appreciation, he loosened his purse strings and gave the new employee several raises. Soon she was making more money than his previous bookkeeper had made. This happy state of affairs continued for some time until the bookkeeper's husband was transferred to an out-of-state position, and she left her job to join him. On her last day in the office, her boss actually cried softly. He held a luncheon in her honor and gave her a substantial bonus check as a going-away gift.

The next bookkeeper who came to work for this man knew nothing of appraising people and situations as good, thereby resurrecting the good in them. She knew nothing of the magic power of praise and approval. The result was that the employer retreated into his shell of unpleasantness and soon regained his title of many years' standing as the hardest man in town to work for.

When you see beauty, life, pleasantness springing up all around in the wonders of nature, use often the resurrecting power of love through praise. Also express approval of others, appraise situations as good regardless of appearances, and glorify your own appearance and your world. As you do so, you will become a part of the resurrecting power of love that is mightily at work in every atom of the universe.

YOU CAN MULTIPLY BEAUTY IN YOUR APPEARANCE AND IN YOUR WORLD

You can glorify your own appearance and that of your world by creating as much beauty as possible. A famous actress was once asked how she stayed so young, though she was actually past seventy. Her reply was that she remained youthful by looking at beauty, appreciating beauty, thinking about beauty.

You can have more beauty in your world if you will begin right where you are to add whatever touches of beauty are possible. As you do this, beauty will multiply in your life. As you dwell more and more on beauty and do all that is possible to produce it in your world, you will become more successful and prosperous.

Once I found myself in a situation where there seemed to be no beauty. One room looked especially hopeless. It was a clutter of old, worn-out, discarded furniture. A friend who knew of the resurrecting power of beauty kept looking at that cluttered room, too. We could not decide what possible use could be made of it, for it seemed so unsightly. Finally we decided to "form a vacuum" by getting rid of all the old furniture, drapes, and rugs.

Almost immediately after the room was emptied, ideas began to come for its redecoration. As the ideas came, we were able to find one item that fitted our redecoration theme. We bought that piece and placed it in the empty room. That one beautiful object was like a magnet. It quickly drew other beautiful objects, as gifts. Money came easily for more costly items to create an elegant atmosphere. Everything and everybody seemed to want to enhance the beauty of that room. Soon it was the most beautiful room in the entire building. People often visited that room just to feed on its beauty. They said it gave them a sense of peace, serenity, well-being. Soon the essence of beauty in that room seemed to permeate the entire building, and redecoration of other rooms took place.

An interior decorator in California wrote:

> The book, *The Prospering Power of Love,* was loaned to me by a friend, and it helped me to solve a knotty business problem.
>
> Now when I speak to groups on interior design, I always read the passage on how the author created a beautiful room. My audiences always love that story! It gives them such hope for beautifying and expanding their own worlds.

You can use this method for accumulating a beautiful wardrobe or for furnishing your home or office. Begin by getting one truly elegant item that delights you and makes you feel rich. If it is an item of clothing, wear it often, mentally appreciating it, and it will open the way for other attractive clothes to be yours.

By fixing your attention on one beautiful item, you create the mental image of beauty, and that image goes to work through you and through others to create more beauty for you. The important thing is to make a start toward beauty, even in a small way. As you do, beauty multiplies for you, and you are able to resurrect beauty and to glorify your life and your world.

THE HEALING POWER OF BEAUTY

Beauty also has resurrecting power for health. When you are trying to achieve freedom from aches and pains, that is the time to wear your brightest, light-colored clothes. The body seems to respond to bright, light colors that suggest life, health, vitality.

Color healing is an ancient science that is now being rediscovered. It was practiced in the healing temples of ancient Egypt, India, and China. Experiments have been carried out in some of our modern hospitals to learn the effect of color on a patient's recovery. Particularly in mental hospitals is color therapy known to be effective.

A schoolteacher, following an automobile accident, broke out with a painful rash that medical treatment failed to alleviate. Someone suggested that she begin giving thanks for its perfect healing in a joyous, happy manner, and that she wear her prettiest, brightest clothes every day until she was healed. It was suggested that instead of staying home and trying to hide the rash, she should get into a party mood and have a good time. It sounded like a ridiculous pre-scription for healing. But it worked.

A woman who had suffered for months with vari-ous aches and pains found that neither medical nor metaphysical treatment seemed to help—until it was suggested that she stop wearing the dark clothes she had worn for months. As she put on light, bright-colored clothes, her body seemed to rejoice in being clothed in beauty, and her aches and pains faded away. She also looked younger, and this helped her mentally to accept a perfect healing. An appropriate affirmation for this purpose is, "I POUR OUT UPON MY BODY TEMPLE THE OIL OF LOVE AND CLOTHE IT IN GARMENTS OF PRAISE."

THERE'S HEALING POWER IN JOY

Another way to glorify your divinity and resurrect your good is through joy. Emma Curtis Hopkins has described the resurrecting power of joy:

> Exaltation is a magnet for all good things of the universe to hasten to you. Depression and anxiety are a magnet for trouble to fly to you. . . . There is no power of healing in a depressed state of mind. . . . In order to work your best, metaphysi-cally, you must be in an exalted state of mind.[*]

---

[*] From *Scientific Christian Mental Practice* by Emma Curtis Hopkins (DeVorss Publications, P.O. Box 1389, Camarillo, CA 93011-1389).

A woman who had experienced great sorrow in her life gave in to despondency, insomnia, and depression. Finally her physician informed her that she would have to overcome her depression, which was affecting her health. He advised her that the way to conquer depression was to laugh at least three times a day, whether she felt like it or not.

Though it seemed ridiculous to follow this advice, she began retiring to her room three time daily for the sole purpose of laughing and making merry, whether there was actually anything to laugh about or not. She was soon in excellent health again, and her previously sorrowful life took on a happy new look.

Charles Fillmore has written: "All healing systems recognize joy as a beneficent factor in the restoration of health to the sick. . . . That there is an intimate relation between happiness and health goes without question."*

A business executive had a sudden attack of acute indigestion. He decided to see if joy would heal him. He had heard a lecturer say, "If you can manage to smile continuously for just five minutes, you can cure any pain." He went to the mirror and stood there smiling, timing himself by his watch to be sure he held the smile for five minutes. By the end of the five minutes, he was so amused at this method that he was laughing aloud. Suddenly he thought of the acute pain he had experienced just five minutes earlier. It was gone!

---

* *Jesus Christ Heals*, by Charles Fillmore (Unity School of Christianity, Unity Village, MO 64065, 1939).

Fun, laughter, and joy are among the world's cheapest and best medicines. Give yourself large doses of these often. They will not only save you expensive medical bills, they will also make your body healthier and your life happier.

JOYOUS ATTITUDES TOWARD OTHERS CAN HEAL THEM

If a person does not know of the resurrecting power of maintaining a joyous, pleasant frame of mind, someone near him can still help resurrect his good by maintaining a joyous attitude about his life and affairs for him.

A popular radio announcer was warned that he would die of a supposedly incurable disease. When the doctors told this to his wife and said he could not possibly live, she replied: "Tell me no more. I refuse to accept that diagnosis. My husband is too fine a man to die. He still has so much to give the world. I have faith that my husband is going to be healed." She continued to maintain this pleasant, faith-filled attitude.

Not only did the man have this disease, but he was also an alcoholic. When relatives and friends tried earlier to console his wife about his drinking, she had not accepted their sympathy. Instead she replied: "My husband is too fine a man to be addicted to alcohol. He is going to be healed."

When her husband was sent home from the hospital, his case diagnosed as hopeless, he and his wife joined a prayer group that believed in spiritual healing. Many of his radio listeners were also praying for his healing. Through consistent prayer, he was healed of both the physical condition and the desire to drink.

A famous television personality learned of the announcer's healing. Since the television star had recently had an operation for the same disease and his future seemed uncertain, he wrote the announcer asking his secret for having made such a successful comeback. The announcer replied: "In the first place, don't believe any diagnosis you are given, unless you are told you can be healed. Refuse to believe anything else. Then pray daily, asking God what it is in life you are really supposed to do, and *joyously* get busy doing it!"

This series of events took place several years ago. Both the radio announcer and the television personality are still well and active in their careers.

YOUR LIFE CAN BECOME AS WONDERFUL AS YOU WANT IT TO BE

Lowell Fillmore once described the resurrecting power of joyous, happy words:

Good words . . . bring happiness and prosperity into our life, while . . . angry words interfere with the digestive processes in our stomach and upset other functions of our body. When you give someone a good tongue-lashing you harm yourself more than you do your target. . . . There is no nourishment in words of criticism concerning evil. . . . Neither can you grow and prosper on hard words. . . . Let your conversation be composed of words that are filled with the constructive vitamins of Spirit. . . . So when you have anything good to say, say it for goodness' sake.

Just as Mother Nature comes alive through the expression of beauty and joy, you can bring back to notice, to use, to life, the divinity within you and your own life through the expression of beauty and joy. Express the resurrecting power of love often by affirming: "THROUGH THE POWER OF CHRIST WITHIN ME, MY LIFE CAN BE AS WONDERFUL AS I WANT IT TO BE! I POUR OUT UPON MY BODY TEMPLE THE OIL OF LOVE AND CLOTHE IT IN GARMENTS OF PRAISE. I APPRAISE OTHERS AS GOOD AS I AFFIRM FOR THEM: 'THROUGH THE POWER OF CHRIST IN YOU, YOUR LIFE CAN BE AS WONDERFUL AS YOU WANT IT TO BE.' I SAY IT FOR GOODNESS' SAKE. AND I GIVE THANKS THAT WE ARE ALL GREAT — GREAT WITH DIVINITY!"

Part II

SPECIAL METHODS OF LOVE

SPECIAL METHODS OF LOVE

Stage I

— Chapter 5 —

One of the basic teachings of Truth is that all environments, circumstances, and conditions we experience existed first as ideas in our own mind, either consciously or subconsciously. One of the great secrets of love is to learn how to clear disharmonious ideas from our own mind, for this in turn clears disharmonious experiences and relationships from our life. *If you deal in the right way with your own thinking, the people around you will move into right conditions—either in your presence or by moving out of your life.* In one way or another, harmony will be established.

I want to share with you a special method for getting your thinking into divine order, promptly and surely. This mystical prayer method can add years to your life, as it relieves you of unnecessary worry and friction. It can work wonders in your relationships with others. It may even turn enemies into friends.

73

And it will surely add immeasurably to your own mental and physical health and wealth.

HOW THIS METHOD WORKS

You can employ this special method of love secretly—with written words. True words are angels. True words are alive with good, and they produce good. But there is a definite method by which you can employ words and produce angelic results: by thinking of the person you are concerned about as having an angel or higher self (spiritual self) to whom you write.

By writing to a person's angel, you establish in your own thinking a harmonious belief about that person. You radiate your harmonious feeling to that person subconsciously; and you also recognize and bring alive in that person's consciousness his or her own higher, spiritual self.

There is special power in writing to the angel of a person you can't help in the usual ways or with whom you cannot reason. *There is something about written words of Truth that reaches to the center of reason of such a person, getting past the emotional blocks of vanity, pride, and deception, and past intellectual argument, and penetrating his or her God-self.*

YOUNG DOCTOR PROVES THIS METHOD

I have known a number of persons who have used this special method of love for reaching troublesome people and clearing up inharmony. A young doctor recently learned of this method. For some months he had been out of harmony with another doctor and had used every means he knew to restore harmony, but the other physician had rebuffed his bids for reconciliation. The young doctor began writing daily to the angel of the other man, asking that perfect understanding be reestablished between them. Later the other doctor met him on the street, greeted him graciously, and invited him to lunch. Now they are again good friends.

RECONCILIATION ACHIEVED
WITH STEPMOTHER

After their parents' divorce, two daughters went to live with their father and new stepmother. For a time it seemed to be a sticky situation, with tension, resentment, and hostility being expressed. These daughters tearfully reported this unhappy situation to their mother, who lived in another state. Her first reaction was one of helplessness and frustration. Then she remembered the miracle power of the angel-writing prayer method, and quietly suggested that her daughters use it.

As they began to write daily to their own angels and to that of their stepmother, the tension and resentment melted away. Words of apology and notes of love were exchanged, followed by hugs and kisses. Happy tears were shed. Later their mother said, "It is a joy to feel the happiness my daughters are now experiencing with their father and stepmother."

A WONDER-WORKING TECHNIQUE

I described this mystical writing-to-the-angel method in an earlier edition of *The Prospering Power of Love,* as well as in my books *The Dynamic Laws of Healing* and *The Dynamic Laws of Prayer.* This secret prayer method can work wonders in your life—and in the lives of others!

I first learned of this secret prayer method from studying the mystical yet practical writings of Emma Curtis Hopkins.* She was known as the "teacher of teachers" in the metaphysical field at the turn of the twentieth century, and she taught this prayer method in her master classes in Chicago, San Francisco, and other cities around the country. Fifty thousand people studied with her in that era, long before radio, television, and other mass-media methods of communication were available. The Fillmores, who founded the Unity movement, were students of Mrs. Hopkins, and the founders of both the Religious Science and Divine Science movements were greatly influenced by her teachings, too.

Dr. H. B. Jeffery, who was reportedly a student of hers, also wrote succinctly of this prayer method in his book, *Mystical Teachings.*† And the Holy Bible contains numerous passages for invoking angel-powers in times of need. Abraham promised: "Jeho-

---

* See her books *Scientific Christian Mental Practice* and *High Mysticism,* both published by DeVorss Publications, P.O. Box 1389, Camarillo, CA 93011-1389.

† *Mystical Teachings,* by H. B. Jeffery (Christ Truth League, Fort Worth, TX 76112-5002, 1954).

vah before whom I walk will send his angel with thee, and prosper thy ways." (Genesis 24:40)

WHEN OTHER PRAYER METHODS HAVE NOT WORKED

All religions and cultures have taught that our word is our power. Many teachings have recognized the special power of written words. The Chinese had such an affection for the written word that they taught for centuries never to tear up a sheet of writing nor to misuse any paper with written words on it, even if it had no further practical use. The Greeks long believed that words are filled with cosmic power, and that one can do anything with words—build or destroy.

A Prayer Method that Worked for a Businessman in Germany: Since I began steadfastly using the angel-writing method of prayer described in *The Prospering Power of Love,* my life has improved in amazing ways.

When I began using this special prayer method, first changes came *within* me, and later, changes began to come in the circumstances of my life. This is especially gratifying since other prayer methods had not worked for me.

PROSPEROUS RESULTS

He Went from Rags to Riches in Europe: Even though I am a professional person, I was living in one room, barely surviving financially. Then I read about the angel-writing method in *The Prospering Power of Love*.

I began to write to my Prosperity Angel, asking its help. Within two years I literally went from "rags to riches." Increased supply came miraculously through my work, and in other ways. *Within three years from the time I began writing to my Prosperity Angel, I was able to retire!*

I now travel worldwide, visiting the great religious shrines, engaging in charity work, and helping others. Truly my Prosperity Angel has become my best friend. I still write to it often and ask its help, both for myself and others. I have also found power in writing to the Prosperity Angel of other people, inviting their own angel to aid them.

How Abundance Came to Her in Arizona: A short while ago I read of how a divorced mother felt she should take her children and move from California to Idaho. Her former husband said if she did he would give her no more child support money. She wrote to his angel and he *did* continue to support their children anyway.

I had a long-standing debt from my former husband for child support he owed us. In reading the above story, I decided to try angel-writing. I wrote to his angel and asked for help.

Two days later I called my former husband and proposed a solution of how he could help me out financially. He gave me more money than I had ever dreamed he would! He was nicer and more agreeable to me than he had ever been. Thanks for enlightening my mind about this mystical yet practical prayer method. *I now use the angel-writing method to solve all kinds of problems.*

Better Job in Wisconsin: A businesswoman was dissatisfied with her job, so she began to write to the angel of her boss, and of her job. Three days later her boss fired her, and she pronounced it good. A week later she had a far better job, more pay, and happier working conditions.

How He Collected Money in Nevada: A realtor reported that he has collected thousands and thousands of dollars from people who would not previously pay him—once he began to write to their angels.

Stolen Property Returned in Texas: We had a brand new truck stolen out of our locked dealership. Instead of getting upset, I wrote to the angel of the person who had taken this truck, asking that person to release it.

A few days later, we received a phone call saying the vehicle had been found abandoned, out of state, with the keys still in the ignition. Except for one dent in the fender, it is in good shape. Our insurance company is taking care of that and having it returned to us. That was fast service—both in inner and outer ways!

In New York, a Minister's Prayer for Her Church Was Answered: Three days after I began writing to the prosperity angel of our church, asking its help, a gentleman came through the door of our sanctuary to invite me, a minister, to move my work into a temple he had just bought.

He had found some of our literature, liked it, and wanted that kind of church housed in his building. I praise God and our prosperity angel for this turn of events—since it frees me from all financial strain so that I can minister on the spiritual level where I am needed so much.

HEALING RESULTS

Healing in Illinois: The friend of a businessman in Chicago was hospitalized, not expected to live. When this businessman learned of his friend's condition, he wrote to the sick man's angel, asking its help in healing him. The next time he heard from the friend, he was not only out of the hospital, but back at work!

Healing of Alcoholism in California: About two years ago I wrote to my ex-husband's angel, asking its help in freeing him from the drinking habit that was ruining his life. It had already ruined our marriage. I asked his angel to help him make peace with our son, who still needed contact with him.

It seemed a big request to make, since my former husband had been an alcoholic since he was fourteen years old. Also at the time I wrote to his angel, my ex-husband had not communicated with me or our son for twelve years.

Nevertheless, two months ago he contacted our son, and we learned that he had stopped drinking just about the time I had written to his angel. My son now has a father he can be proud of, after so many years of having none. What a wonderfully effective prayer method the angel-writing technique is. I only wish people everywhere knew about it. What a different world this could be.

Lady in Virginia Loses Twenty Pounds: A couple of years ago I decided to write to my angel concerning a weight problem. I was very enthusiastic about it, and through that method, I lost twenty pounds.

Rehabilitation from Drugs for a Vietnam Veteran in New York: Since we began writing to his angel, my son has gone on a drug rehabilitation program and is doing fine. Considering the physical and mental condition he has been in since he returned from the war, this is a miracle. He has gone to work for the government—another miracle.

HAPPY RESULTS IN RELATIONSHIPS

Family Harmonized in Africa: I wrote to my wife's angel when she was filled with resentment and criticism. She has responded positively ever since. My son has become more harmonious, too, as a result of this special prayer method.

Hostility Dissolved in Illinois: The angel-writing prayer method really works. We had been trying to get help in paying our hospital bills, and the man we spoke to was very hostile. I wrote to his angel asking its help, and the next time I spoke to him he had completely changed. *I have also been busy writing daily to our own angels of prosperity, healing, love and marriage, and we are seeing notable improvement on all levels of our lives.*

Lawsuit Dropped in Texas: A businesswoman learned that a lawsuit was being filed against her, very unfairly. She had been a victim of circumstances in which someone else was responsible, yet she was being blamed for the mix-up and being sued. It was very frustrating until she remembered to write to the angel of the situation, asking that the legal matter be cleared up quickly and in peace. Things suddenly got very quiet after they had been most unpleasant. The quietness continued for several weeks. Then she learned that the lawsuit had been dropped.

A Memorable Mother's Day in Pennsylvania:
The biggest piece of happiness which has come my
way in a long time is that I got to spend Mother's
Day with my son and daughter. Because of a previously bitter divorce action, to see them again
seemed a miracle. We went to the movies in the afternoon, and spent a leisurely dinner together. My
son gave me a book and a card signed "love." I now
look at that card daily. He even leaned over the table and kissed me. My daughter gave me a potted
plant.

We had a pleasant, relaxed three-hour dinner together in a restaurant. It was such a happy time. I
looked up the entry made in my diary on Mother's
Day last year, and it was a barren, lonely day for
me. This one was in direct contrast. It still makes
me happy to think about it. I shall continue dwelling
on "divine love" and writing to the angels of all
concerned.

WRITE TO A SPECIFIC ANGEL
TO MEET A SPECIFIC NEED

If writing to a person's angel in a general way
does not seem to get results, sometimes it is more
powerful to get specific, and to write to the angel of
that person's particular need: such as writing to the
Angel of Protection, the Angel of Healing, the Angel
of Love and Marriage, the Angel of Harmony and
Happiness, the Angel of Wisdom and Guidance, the

Angel of Prosperity and Wealth, or the Angel of Spiritual Growth and Understanding.

THE ANGEL OF DIVINE PROTECTION

Before traveling or going forth into any challenging situation, it is wise to declare: "THE ANGEL OF DIVINE PROTECTION GOES BEFORE ME, SHIELDING ME FROM ANY NEGATIVE EXPERIENCES" or "THE ANGEL OF DIVINE PROTECTION GOES BEFORE ME AND PREPARES MY WAY." The prophet Malachi might have been speaking of his angel-protector when he said, "Behold, I send my messenger, and he shall prepare the way before me." (Malachi 3:1)

Two missionaries were passing through a dangerous jungle region where robbers were waiting to attack them. But as the missionaries approached, they prayed for divine protection. The robbers saw a "third person," much larger than life-size, traveling with the missionaries and apparently guarding them. The presence of this third party, or Angel of Protection, both puzzled and frightened the robbers, so the missionaries were saved from harm.

THE ANGEL OF HEALING

The Hebrews of old felt that Raphael was the Angel of Healing. At times you may wish to decree and/or write out: "ANGEL OF HEALING, COME FORTH HERE AND NOW."

A story appeared in the newspapers in England many years ago about a woman who had been ill for five years and was dying from an advanced physical condition. Doctors had long despaired of saving her, and relatives had gathered round as she stopped breathing and appeared to be gone. Minutes later, she suddenly took a deep breath and roused, as she said conversationally, "Yes, I am listening. Who is it?" At that moment those in the room saw an angel bending over her sickbed and replying, "Your sufferings are over. Get up and walk."

When she asked for her robe, it caused a great commotion, because she had been bedridden for months. She then walked into another room and asked for food, though she had not had a solid meal for months.

After five years of intense suffering, she quickly regained her health, and medical tests revealed there was not a trace of the disease left in her body. Thereafter, she ate well, slept well, and was quite calm and peaceful. Nothing seemed to tire or excite her. The angel had told her that her life was being spared so she might help to heal others. After that, she spent a great deal of time in intercessory prayer for the sick in her village, asking the Angel of Healing to make them whole. Her life took on new meaning and satisfaction as many healings occurred.

THE ANGEL OF PROSPERITY

Once when I was planning a six-week lecture trip, I decided to test the angel prayer-method by asking that the Angel of Prosperity go before me, making prosperous and successful my way. When I was lecturing for business or convention groups, a professional lecture fee was often in order. But the offerings

I received when lecturing in churches were sometimes so small they did not pay my expenses—and
this was to be a lecture trip for churches.

However, on this trip, after sending the Angel of
Prosperity before me, something happened that had
never happened before: along the way people kept
saying privately, "I have read your books and have
been helped by them. I want to show my appreciation
by sharing a special tithe offering with you." The result was that I went home carrying a number of tithe
checks as special gifts to me personally. They helped
to defray costs I so often had to meet on my own.

THE ANGEL OF WEALTH

A businessman recently wrote: "I came out of financial limitation and despair by writing to my Prosperity Angel daily. But then I kept waiting to go further: from general prosperity to definite wealth. That
did not happen until I got more specific and began to
write to the Angel of Wealth. Now, at last, I am financially independent."

THE ANGEL OF RELEASE

If you have been unable to gain release from
health, financial, human relations, or other types of
problems, writing to the Angel of Freedom and Release can be very effective, too. Once when I had
been unable to gain freedom from some people who I
felt were using me in a number of ways, I began
writing to the Angel of Release, asking its help. I was
soon shown how to claim my freedom, and I was able

to gain complete release from them. This newfound freedom soon proved to be a blessing to all concerned. "The good of one was the good of all."

Special Note: To receive a free copy of the author's "How to Write to the Angel" outline, please send your request to P.O. Drawer 1278, Palm Desert, CA 92261 USA.

SPECIAL METHODS OF LOVE

Stage II

— Chapter 6 —

John, in his Revelation, speaks of writing to the angels of the seven churches. (Revelation 1:19, 20) The word "church" most often symbolizes spiritual consciousness. The seven churches are symbolic of the seven types of people whom we can best reach spiritually by writing to their angels or higher selves in specific ways. These may be people we have seemed unable to reach in other ways—whether through our general prayers for them or through writing to their angels of healing, prosperity, love, wealth, or release, as described in the previous chapter.

FIRST: HOW TO REACH
THE EXCITABLE TYPE

"To the angel of the church in Ephesus write . . ." (Revelation 2:1)

The word "Ephesus" means "desirable, appealing." You may know desirable or appealing people — who are nevertheless hard to reach. Their outward life is full of excitement. They are emotional, lovers of amusement, theatrical in their tastes, dramatic in everything they do. Paul spent three years preaching Truth in Ephesus, because he realized such people were hard to reach and help.

The wonderful thing to remember about those in this category whom you are trying to help is that they have an intense desire for greater good in their lives. Though they may seem restless or anxious, they are easy to know, pleasant and agreeable, and they are interested in the finer things of life. By writing to their angels and stating the Truth about them, you easily reach that deeper aspect of their nature, and they happily respond.

A friend of mine was a fine person of this type. He was an emotional man with an exciting life and a flair for the dramatic. He owed me for some work I had done for his firm. Several months passed and I had not been paid. My affirmations had brought no results.

Finally I remembered the angel-writing technique, and late one night I quietly wrote, "TO THE ANGEL OF [let us say 'John Brown']. I BLESS YOU AND GIVE THANKS THAT YOU ARE HANDLING THIS FINANCIAL MATTER PROMPTLY, AND THAT I AM IMMEDIATELY AND COMPLETELY PAID." (I wrote this statement fifteen times, because many mystics believed fifteen is the number that dissolves adversity and hard conditions.)

After writing out the statement, I felt much better about the situation and was able to release it completely from my mind. Two days later, my friend telephoned to say that I would receive the payment by mail the following day—and I did!

SECOND: HOW TO REACH
THE BITTER-SWEET TYPE

*"And to the angel of the church
in Smyrna write . . ."* (Revelation 2:8)

The word "Smyrna" means "flowing substance." Smyrnians present a fine appearance. They are lovers of show, beauty, adornment. They live beyond their means and usually have financial problems.

A businessman was having great difficulty with his wife, who had divorced him. He was heartbroken because he still loved her. He had tried to talk with her about reconciliation, but she was very confused, and he could not reason with her.

He learned of this special method of love and was fascinated with the idea, realizing that his wife was this second type. She was an attractive lady, and loved fine things. In fact, that had been one of their basic problems: her tastes had been much too expensive for his pocketbook.

He began writing each night to her angel, asking for help in straightening out their relationship. One day, after he had not heard from her for some time, she contacted him, tearfully declaring that their divorce had been a mistake. Soon they were remarried. This man has found it possible to maintain peace and harmony with his wife by continuing to write to her angel.

THIRD: HOW TO REACH
THE ALOOF, INTELLECTUAL TYPE

"And to the angel of the church
in Pergamum write . . ." (Revelation 2:12)

The word "Pergamum" means "strongly united, closely knit." These are the grand, often wealthy, aristocratic types—literary, scientific, artistic, lovers of society and statecraft, strongly united, closely knit in family, social, and business relationships. These persons may be suspicious of strangers, new friends, new ideas.

A young man fell in love and wanted to marry. But the girl of his choice was from a closely-knit family that did not want to release her emotionally. This family group was suspicious of new people, new ways of doing things, and all new ideas. In fact, they were strongly united against the invasion of *anything* new in their lives.

The young man realized that from a human standpoint, it seemed hopeless to try to win the girl because of her strong family ties, even though she was in love with him. Being a Truth student, he reasoned that the only possible way to deal with the possessiveness of her family was through the practice of love.

At this point, he learned of love's special method. He wrote to the girl's angel and to the angel of her family, decreeing her emotional freedom, a happy marriage, and a family divinely adjusted to this change. For some months, he continued this angel-writing technique, with no visible results. Then suddenly everything changed. He could sense a freedom that had not previously existed. He proposed, and they were soon married. Though it took her family some time to adjust to the change and to accept him emotionally into the family, they finally did so wholeheartedly.

FOURTH: HOW TO REACH
THE ZEALOUS, QUARRELSOME TYPE

*"And to the angel of the church
of Thyatira write . . ."* (Revelation 2:18)

"Thyatira" means "rushing headlong, frantic, zealous, quarrelsome, easily offended." People of this type have ideas that are greater than their inner ability to produce the idealistic results they desire. Thyatirans are quite often interested in athletics.

A housewife learned that the instructor at a health club was being harsh with the teenage boys he was instructing. Though her son and his friends were upset by this harsh treatment, they did not wish her to interfere, feeling that would bring only more scorn from their instructor. The mother asked the boys to begin writing to the angel of their instructor, decreeing fair treatment and understanding. She joined them in their angel-writing project.

For a time no results were apparent. Suddenly, however, the instructor announced he was leaving his job to take a better position with a local college. Along with providing an increased income, the new job would allow him time to work on his master's degree, which had long been his desire. The mother then realized that the young instructor's harsh treatment apparently had stemmed from his own frustration and job dissatisfaction. The amazing result was that this woman's son later won a trophy from the health club—a trophy topped with the figure of an angel!

FIFTH: HOW TO REACH
THE FEARFUL, BODY-DEVOTEE TYPE

*"And to the angel of the church
in Sardis write . . ."* (Revelation 3:1)

The word "Sardis" means "prince of power, timid, apprehensive, always fearful about something." These people are body devotees. They are afraid of drafts, accidents, what they eat. They are always seeking the comfortable, soft, pleasant things of bodily life. No books, lessons, or instructions seem to quench their fears, but writing to their angels uplifts the bold, brave, dauntless spirit in them, and they become "princes of power."

These types of people are always changing their minds. The throat, which is a power center in the body, is usually a weak spot. They may develop a sore throat or some other throat ailment when they become fearful.

Such persons have great potential for becoming powerful individuals. You can awaken that power center within them and bring it alive through writing to their angel. This gives them a stability and fearlessness they desire to express.

A businessman was once having difficulty trying to bring a matter to a conclusion. It had been pending for a long time. Everyone involved was congenial and wished to conclude negotiations except one person, who kept changing his mind. This person seemed unsure about every aspect of the matter.

The businessman heard of the angel-writing method and realized that the man who kept changing his mind was timid, apprehensive, fearful, unsure. He wrote to the man's angel, asking that the business matter be brought to an early, appropriate conclusion, so all involved would be satisfied and blessed.

A few days later, the man who had stalled for a long time said, "Come down to my office tomorrow morning and the papers will be ready to sign." Then he added, as though it were his idea, "This situation has been delayed long enough, and I am anxious to conclude it."

SIXTH: HOW TO REACH
THE LOVING-WORKS TYPE

"And to the angel of the church
in Philadelphia write . . ." (Revelation 3:7)

The word "Philadelphia" means "brotherly love, fraternal love, universal love." People of this type talk much about the brotherhood of man, but love to them usually means outer works alone, and not necessarily an inner consciousness of love. These are the philanthropists. Community organizations, clubs, fraternal groups, civic groups, and churches are all filled with people seeking brotherly love, universal love. They sometimes become frustrated through exhausting themselves in loving works.

If you find yourself in a group or organization where the loving works do not seem to be balanced by an inner consciousness of love, you can write to the angel of that organization, asking that divine love come alive in the thoughts as well as in the actions of the group. As you do, those people who are not in tune with divine love will fade harmoniously out of the group, and those who are lovingly in tune with its aims and purposes will appear. In this secret, quiet way, both inner and outer harmony can be established and maintained.

An executive found himself in the midst of organizational disharmony. He was not sure just who was responsible for the unrest and critical attitudes in the group. He tried various methods for reestablishing harmony, but the group remained aloof, critical, disharmonious.

In desperation, he began writing daily to the angel of that organization, asking for help in reestablishing a consciousness of love. Then he wrote: "I CAST THIS BURDEN ON THE ANGEL OF DIVINE LOVE. THE ANGEL OF LOVE NOW COMES ALIVE IN THIS SITUATION AND IN ALL PERSONS CONNECTED WITH THIS ORGANIZATION. THE ANGEL OF DIVINE LOVE NOW REIGNS SUPREME."

Soon several volunteer workers resigned their jobs, leaving the organization, and new workers appeared who were eager to contribute to the progress of the organization in a harmonious way. Peace and progress were established and maintained.

SEVENTH: HOW TO REACH
THE UNSETTLED TYPE

*"And to the angel of the church
in Laodicea write . . ."* (Revelation 3:14)

The word "Laodicea" means "justice and judgment." People of this type often have an injustice complex. They are unsettled, changeable wanderers seeking new doctrines and new places. They often change their religious beliefs and their political views. They are restless, critical. They usually feel they have been wronged or misused.

You find this type of person going from one job to another, from one church to another, from one club to another. They are the "joiners" who do not remain with anything long enough to discover whether it will benefit them or not.

When you write to the angel of such persons, decree that the divine law of love and justice is doing its perfect work in their life and affairs, and that they are being divinely guided into their right place. They will subconsciously respond more and more to your high vision of rightness and stability for them.

WRITE TO YOUR OWN ANGEL

In writing to another's angel, it may appear that nothing is being accomplished. Then, suddenly, everything will shift, changes will come, and matters that had seemed destined for failure will clear up very quickly. But sometimes one must practice patience before this happens.

The word *angel* means "messenger of God." *The Metaphysical Bible Dictionary** explains: "The office of the angels is to guard and guide and direct the natural forces of mind and body, which have in them the future of the whole man." Do not fail to write to your own angel when it seems that your life is filled with defeat or when you are tempted to criticize and condemn yourself.

Emma Curtis Hopkins writes:

> The Angel of His Presence accompanies every man. . . . This high leadership is every man's heritage. He need not fear dangerous days or vicious circumstances while he is aware that his angel goes before him, pleads his cause and defends him.[†]

When challenges arise, say to yourself: "I HAVE NOTHING TO FEAR. MY GUARDIAN ANGEL GOES BEFORE ME, MAKING RIGHT MY WAY." Decree it for others. A businesswoman was concerned about having to make an out-of-town buying trip, which required that she drive two hundred miles in rain and fog, accompanied by her ailing husband, whom she could not leave at home alone. A friend said, "You have nothing to fear, because your guardian angel will be with you."

Upon returning from the buying trip, she said to her friend: "It *did* seem that we were accompanied by

---

[*] *The Metaphysical Bible Dictionary* (Unity School of Christianity, Unity Village, MO 64065, 1931).

[†] *High Mysticism,* by Emma Curtis Hopkins (DeVorss Publications, P.O. Box 1389, Camarillo, CA 93011-1389).

an angel. As I drove out of town, within a few minutes the sky cleared of fog, the rain stopped, and the sun shone through. There was no more bad weather on the entire trip. The drive helped my husband's spirits and he suffered no ill effects from it. Financially, this proved to be the most profitable buying trip I have made in a long time."

ANGEL-WRITING PRODUCES
NEITHER HURT NOR HARM

Never expect your angel or that of another to honor any requests that might hurt or harm. Be willing that something infinitely better than that which you think you want will come as you use love's special method. This will open the way for your good and for the good of all involved to manifest in an unlimited, satisfying manner.

For invoking love's special method, meditate often upon the promise of the Psalmist:

There shall no evil befall thee, neither shall any plague come nigh thy dwelling. For he shall give his angels charge over thee, to keep thee in all thy ways. (Psalms 91:10, 11)

HOW LOVE PROSPERS

— Chapter 7 —

I must admit that the first time I read these words written by Charles Fillmore in his book *Prosperity,*[*] I was skeptical about their practical value:

> Tell me what kind of thoughts you are holding about yourself and your neighbors and I can tell you just what you may expect in the way of health, finances, and harmony. . . . You cannot love and trust in God if you hate and distrust men. The two ideas, love and hate, or trust and mistrust, simply cannot both be present in your mind at one time, and when you are entertaining one, you may be sure the other is absent. Trust other people and use the power that you accumulate from that act to trust God. There is magic in it: it works wonders; love and trust are dynamic, vital powers.

---

[*] *Prosperity,* by Charles Fillmore (Unity School of Christianity, Unity Village, MO 64065).

These words are in his chapter on indebtedness. I could not imagine love having anything to do with debt!

LOVE DISSOLVES DEBT
FOR A BUSINESSMAN

But love *does* have something to do with the dissolution of indebtedness. The owner of a furniture company in Alabama once related one of his many experiences along this line:

This man had a customer who refused to pay for a washing machine purchased from his store. The finance company finally reclaimed it, then the customer came rushing into the furniture store and started screaming at the proprietor in vile language. This raging man weighed nearly two hundred forty pounds and he stood about six feet three inches tall, whereas the store owner was a much smaller man. As the customer made his abusive accusations, the furniture dealer listened quietly. Whenever possible, he declared softly between accusations, "But [naming the man], I love you!" He made this statement dozens of times until finally the enraged customer left in utter disgust.

In about thirty minutes, he returned to apologize for his behavior and to thank the furniture store owner for the way he had dealt with the situation. The customer then explained that he had lost his last job because of his temper, which had caused him to assault a man who later had to be hospitalized.

He further stated that the way the dealer had handled the situation turned the tide of his temper and made him see how foolish he had been. He promised that as soon as he found another job he would pay for the washing machine—and he did. He became a fine, stable customer of this dealer, who acknowledges that it was not easy to say "I love you" to another man, especially a raging one, but declared that he had found it well worth the effort.

LAWYER USES LOVE
TO COLLECT MONEY

A lawyer who had also studied Charles Fillmore's book *Prosperity* once related that he collected two big accounts by releasing love and trust as dynamic, vital powers.

At the end of that particular year, in going over his books, he found two especially large accounts still due. He recalled that Mr. Fillmore had written, "A thought of debt will produce debt." He reasoned that as long as he believed in debt, resented debt, or attached the thought of debt to himself or others, he would remain in debt. So, to overcome such negative thoughts and also to invoke the power of love and trust, the lawyer made a mental note of the clients who owed him large amounts. He began blessing their names daily, each one separately, and sincerely erasing the idea of debt attached to each one.

After he had been using this system for a short time, the two clients who owed these large sums settled with him on the same day, one of them mailing his check for the full amount from a distant state.

HOW THEY USED LOVE TO PROSPER

I no longer doubt Charles Fillmore's claims on the power of love to prosper oneself and others. I have discovered it is true: love and trust *are* dynamic, vital powers which seem to contain magic energies that can work wonders in your life. The following are but a few of the reports I have received from readers over the years that clearly indicate this:

First Vacation in Eight Years in Ohio: I had not had a vacation in eight years when I began to declare, "DIVINE LOVE FORESEES EVERYTHING AND RICHLY PROVIDES EVERYTHING NOW."

A friend soon presented me the gift of a round-trip ticket to Florida. Another friend invited me to share her hotel accommodations while she was there on a business trip. The only cost I had was my meals. This vacation was such a blessing to me.

Better Living Arrangements in California: After I began to daily use "divine love" statements, miracles happened. A friend soon invited me to move into her home, and use her spare bedroom. Our sharing of expenses has cut them in half. I sold most of my old furniture in just four days—another miracle. The income from this sale has helped tide me over until some income that was pending is released. "The prospering power of love" has worked for me!

How He Passed Realtor's Exam in Massachusetts: I took a most difficult and tricky real estate examination. This particular test, designed to eliminate the maximum number of candidates, also required memorizing one hundred and fifty pages of legal data.

I dislike reading textbooks and my eyes glazed over whenever I tried to study for the exam. Furthermore, I had not taken any exam for forty years, and never one of this type—which required so much memory work and accuracy. But I remembered reading that a person should pour love into whatever he does. I did, and I passed!

Cabinet Shop Prospers in New York: Since we began to use "divine love" statements, work has poured into our cabinet shop. We got so busy that we had to hire another employee, who is very helpful. Love *is* prospering us.

A Single Parent Prospered in the West Indies: Since first studying *The Prospering Power of Love,* I have often used divine-love affirmations to help me meet my needs, and the good has always come—sometimes in miraculous ways.

I did not have a cent, yet with the help of divine love, I was able to purchase a $4000 car. My children and I had long needed a car, but as a single parent I had felt we should not attempt it. After food, clothes and rent, there was little left. I had no savings except what I gave to God's work in tithes. I called this my "spiritual bank."

When my cousin said she was getting a new car, I asked her to consider holding her old one for me. At home the children and I began to declare: "DIVINE LOVE NOW PROVIDES US WITH THE MONEY TO BUY THE PERFECT CAR FOR US, AND TO PAY FOR IT WITHOUT STRAIN."

I was then able to borrow $500 from a small insurance policy and $500 from a friend. But the bank would not accept this amount because, for a used car, they required one-half in cash. My cousin said she would hold the car for me, although she had several cash offers on it.

The children agreed with me that "DIVINE LOVE IS IN CHARGE AND THE BEST WILL HAPPEN." In spite of my disappointment, I was able to release the matter to divine love. When I did, my cousin delivered the car to me, and said I could begin making payments when my loan arrangements had been satisfactorily worked out. So we had the car in time for summer holidays.

Divine love came through for us. At work I soon got a new salary agreement with back pay of $2500, and a raise of $350 per month. So I was able to make the down payment and monthly car payments without strain, as we had affirmed. It is such a joy to prosper with the help of divine love.

Love Cuts Prices in California: It's true that plants respond to love. For weeks, I had admired a certain potted plant at the supermarket, but the price did not fit into my budget. Yet I thought of that plant often with much affection.

Last Saturday as I shopped, I again looked at that plant, thinking how much I would like to have it in my home. Just as I was turning away, a clerk walked by and said, "We're reducing the plants on this shelf to ninety-nine cents today." Zap. Love cuts prices!

DIVINE LOVE CAN MEET EVERY NEED

A long-time friend has often said, "Divine love always has and always will meet every need." Yes, it will, when we give it our attention.

Love to the Rescue in Michigan: I was on the way home after teaching a class sixty miles away. There was snow on the side of the road, but I was not aware of ice on the road. It was 1:00 A.M. and I was whizzing along when suddenly the car landed in a snowbank up to the floor of the car, and up to my knees when I got out of the car.

I started walking up the road in the dark declaring, "I CALL FORTH DIVINE LOVE TO PERFORM ANY MIRACLE NEEDED IN THIS SITUATION NOW."

Within—not minutes, but moments—a man arrived in a van. He had a CB radio, a four-wheel drive, a chain and the "know how" to get my car out of that snowbank. Within fifteen minutes from the time I skidded, I was on my way home. The only damage to my car was a dented left door.

When I had called forth divine love to work a miracle for me at 1:00 A.M. in the dark in a snow-bank, it did! This was a magnificent experience for me in the wonder-working power of love.

He Meets Prison Experience Victoriously in Pennsylvania: I have been granted commutation of my life sentence. The board followed the recommendation of the institution staff that I should serve five more years before being considered for parole.

I was disappointed with this decision, but not discouraged. I shall continue my relationship with God, and do the best I can to compensate for my regrettable crime. I shall continue to use prayer statements on divine love from *The Prospering Power of Love* in order to meet my prison experiences victoriously.

Divine Love Helps Her to Relocate in America: "Divine love" affirmations have worked miracles in my life. Although I am new in this country, I already have a flock of friends and even a prayer partner.

How She Got Married and Stayed Married in Oregon: I decided last year I was not going to let this good way of thinking and living pass me by. I wanted to get married and got very specific on my prayer list about the qualities I desired in a husband. I used "divine love" statements daily.

We met in June and were married in January. I have never been happier in my whole life. This marriage is the best thing that could have happened to me. When there have been adjustments to make in our marriage, I have used "divine love" affirmations and have studied *The Prospering Power of Love*. Any difficulties have always disappeared. *Divine love has worked a miracle in my life, and I am convinced it can do the same for anyone else who will call on it!*

Love Was Soul-Stretching in North Carolina: Divine love works in mysterious ways. I took the best from two adverse marriages. "The best" was two fine children that came through challenging experiences which seemed insurmountable at the time. Through those "soul-stretching" episodes, there has come great spiritual growth within me. I feel there is emerging a more purified and refined nature. My children are doing well in high school and college, and I am now active in a study group which I find inspiring.

LOVE IS RELEASED
THROUGH THE PROSPERING TENTH

Several decades ago, when I came into the ministry out of the business world, a lovely lady minister with whom I worked briefly asked me to help with her correspondence. When she saw some of the letters I prepared, she said, "These are fine, but put some love into them."

In answering her mail I had observed the letter of the law, but had overlooked including the spirit of love.

Putting God first financially on a regular, consistent basis is a sure way to release the prospering power of love—provided you deliberately put love into your acts of giving. Be sure to tithe with love. People sometimes tithe to observe the letter of the law, but do not reap its full benefits when they have not done so in a spirit of love.*

It is easy to put love into your giving when you realize that the first tenth of all you receive belongs to God anyway, and that you are merely returning to Him the sacred tenth of all He has and is giving to you. "The tenth is holy unto Jehovah." (Leviticus 27:32)

This realization takes the fear and resentment out of giving. Instead, it puts love of God and appreciation for His many blessings into your acts of sharing. "Thou shalt remember Jehovah thy God, for it is He that giveth thee power to get wealth." (Deuteronomy 8:18)

---

* Chapters on tithing may be found in the following books by the author: *The Prosperity Secret of the Ages, The Dynamic Laws of Healing, Dare to Prosper!, The Prospering Power of Prayer, Open Your Mind to Prosperity, Open Your Mind to Receive, The Secret of Unlimited Prosperity, The Millionaires of Genesis, The Millionaire Moses, The Millionaire Joshua, The Millionaire from Nazareth,* and *The Dynamic Laws of Prosperity.*

THE SECRET OF FINANCIAL INCREASE

The word "tithe" means "tenth." Since ancient times, "ten" has been considered the magic number of increase. All great civilizations and cultures have taught and practiced the tithing law of prosperity. They have felt that by returning a tenth of all they received to their Creator, they would become attuned to the wisdom and wealth of the universe. Tithing, as an act of spiritual worship and as an act for invoking universal abundance, has been practiced since the time of primitive man.

As the Hebrews of old proved, to tithe is to prosper. In more recent times, the man considered by many to be America's first billionaire was a tither. John D. Rockefeller's total tithes for the year 1855 were $9.50. By 1934, his tithes had grown to a total of $531 million! He often commented, "God gave me my wealth."[*]

Sharing is the beginning of financial increase, as was pointed out by the prophet:

> Bring ye the whole tithe into the storehouse, that there may be food in my house, and prove me now herewith saith Jehovah of hosts, if I will not open you the windows of heaven, and pour you out a blessing, that there shall not be room enough to receive it. (Malachi 3:10)

---

[*] Numerous additional stories about tithing and its amazing results can be found in various of the author's books (see list in previous footnote).

As time goes by, faithful tithers will find themselves remarkably blessed, just as Malachi promised. In fact, those who have followed his advice on a regular basis, practicing systematic tithing, have usually found that the time came when they had more to "share and to spare" than they had previously dreamed possible!

THE COUNTLESS BLESSINGS
OF TITHING

Of all of life's universal laws that I have written about over the years, the tithing law of prosperity seems to be the one that most fascinates people, probably because it carries with it an ancient heritage of success. *I receive more mail on the subject of tithing than on all the other prosperity laws combined!*

Here are just a few reports of the countless blessings that the practice of tithing has brought:

Anxiety about Money Is Gone in California: At first I resented the subject of tithing. But I soon realized that any prosperity law that had made millionaires of the Hebrews of old, and so many people since, was worth trying.

When I began to tithe, all the anxiety about financial matters that had been with me so long left! I have felt guided, protected, safer, calmer. *More than any other single prosperity technique, tithing has changed my life.*

A Loser Became a Winner in Texas: I now have a new rock home in one of the most beautiful neighborhoods of our city. I recently bought a lake lot on which to build a vacation house. I now own my own office building, and my practice is doing well. Tithing has turned this former loser into a winner.

Income Tripled in Less than a Year in Missouri: Looking at my financial records has reminded me that my income has tripled in less than one year, since I began tithing! The act of giving makes me feel so rich.

How He Avoided Problems in New York: I feel sorry for those people who are too indifferent to tithing so that they hold on tightly to every cent. The result is that they find themselves in unpleasant situations, spending far more money than the tithe in an effort to get freed of annoying, unwanted experiences which they would not have had in the first place had they put God first financially. To tithe is the easier way to succeed, and I give thanks I found it.

Why Her Tithing Was Not Productive in Illinois: I tithed in the past, but felt I wasn't supposed to expect anything in return (even though the Bible clearly said I *should*)—so, of course, I did not receive the blessings due me. And I stopped tithing in 1973.

I feel much happier now that I know it is normal and right to expect the Biblical prosperity promises about tithing to be fulfilled for me. It suddenly becomes a joy to give. After studying the tithing law of prosperity further, it has become clear to me why I had those accidents, and all those aches and pains. Since pledging with God to pay my tithes regularly, the pain has diminished and my future looks bright.

A Widow Prospers in Pennsylvania: I have been widowed for eight years. I live in my own home, and I receive $260 per month Social Security. But I gladly share my tithes. I have begun to give in every way that is revealed to me in order to make room to receive more. It works! A lovely trip came to me from my son and his wife. We drove through the state of Virginia this fall. Now my granddaughter has arranged for me to fly to New Mexico to spend a month, with relatives coming to visit from Arizona and Montana.

A Divorcee Makes a New Start in Nevada: Shortly after my divorce, my parents introduced me to *The Prospering Power of Love*. But I was not yet ready to accept the peace and prosperity that were mine to claim. Tithing was one part of Dr. Ponder's teachings that I had difficulty accepting. Instead, I continued in a state of financial struggle and fruitless mental effort.

Finally, when I had only $25 left and did not know where the next cent was coming from with which to provide for my children, I decided to tithe. I realized that putting God first financially was something I must do if I wished to prosper and succeed in life on a permanent and stable basis. The next day I received $190 which was a bonus from the company I left three months previously. I feel that I shall now go forward into a far more prosperous life than I have ever known. This is my spiritual heritage and I am claiming it.

Changing Where She Gave Her Tithe Brought Results in Arizona: I found myself resentful of giving to a congregation with which I no longer had a spiritual affinity, and which I had outgrown. I now give to the church where I get my spiritual help and inspiration, and I have prospered accordingly.

YOU DESERVE NOTHING LESS!

May the foregoing experiences of others inspire you to invoke the prospering power of love through putting God first financially—thereby opening the way for the increase of abundant, permanent good in every phase of your life. As Malachi pointed out, you deserve nothing less!

THE SIX SURPRISES

Furthermore, you may have at least six surprises when you tithe. (1) You will be surprised at the amount of money you have for the Lord's work. (2) You will be surprised at the deepening of your spiritual understanding. (3) You will be surprised at the ease with which you can meet your own obligations. (4) You will be surprised at the ease with which you can go from one-tenth to larger giving. (5) You will be surprised at the way tithing prepares you to be a faithful and wise steward of the remaining nine-tenths. (6) And you will be especially surprised at yourself for not having adopted the tithing method of prosperity sooner!

Part III

SPECIAL LESSONS IN LOVE

From My Three Mothers

THE TWO WHO WANTED ME AND THE ONE
WHO DID NOT . . .

INTRODUCTION

I have been fortunate to have had three mothers: two who wanted me and one who did not. I learned much-needed lessons in love from all of them, as related herein.

It has been said that everyone we meet in life is our teacher. But the lessons we do or don't learn from them are up to us. Every experience can become a lesson and a blessing. Moreover, "Our lives are shaped by those who love us, and by those who refuse to love us."

MY FIRST MOTHER:
The "Martha"

Chapter 8

Like the Master Teacher, I was blessed to have both a Mary and a Martha in my life.

My natural mother—who was with me at the beginning of my life and again much later, at the end of hers—was the "Martha." She did everything for me outwardly that a traditional mother was expected to do.

She provided my meals and sewed my homemade dresses (often made from feed sacks). She drilled me in my homework, prepared my school lunchbox, and went to bat for me at school when I goofed. She nursed my ailments, real and imagined, and she acted as an intermediary in family relationships. Most of all, she unwittingly caused me to discover the inspirational literature she scattered around the house—and meant for my father. But it was also destined to gradually change the course of my life—big time.

As a young widow who was also a single parent (before that term was even invented or appreciated), I was able to leave my young son in her loving care while I worked.

HER TALENTS AND CREDENTIALS

For many years, she was active in our community. She was president of the PTA and was elected as the first lady Elder ever to serve in her Protestant denomination. She was also a regular visitor to shut-ins and the sick in nursing homes and a good neighbor to those who were more underprivileged in our community than we were.

At home, she was usually in the kitchen or at the sewing machine. If she wasn't there, she was busy tending her flowers and vegetables in the yard. I never remember seeing my mother sit down to just relax. She was always on the go. Neither do I remember ever hearing her say "I love you" to anyone—including me. But I'm sure she felt her actions spoke louder than words. Regardless, she was one of the most beloved and respected women in our community. And we, her children, knew we could count on her to come to our rescue, no matter what the situation.

WHEN HER PACE SLOWED

The time came years later, when my father had gone on to the next plane of life. My sister and brother were busy with their own families out of state, and mother's pace had slowed.

After praying about it for a long period, I invited her to move three thousand miles from the East Coast to the West to live near me. I had always hoped the day would come when I would be able to show my appreciation for all she had done years earlier for me and my son.

Thus, for the last twelve years of her life she lived quietly and comfortably at Palm Desert Country Club, where she once again enjoyed flowers and a vegetable garden (this time year-round), as well as fresh fruit in her yard, and the beauty and mild climate of Southern California.

She also enjoyed spending holidays in my guest house and celebrating holiday festivities with me at home and in various private clubs, and she relished our vacations all over the West.

But most of all I think she enjoyed having the company of her first-born child (me) and occasional visits from out-of-state from her first-born grandchild (my son)—after she had been away from us for so many years.

Two days after celebrating a Fourth of July luncheon at my house, she was suddenly gone—in her sleep of natural causes, at the tender age of eighty-five. After a long, healthy life that included years of family and community activities, her transition from this plane of existence bespoke her own private "declaration of independence" in a way that was typical of my mother—a feisty, independent soul from start to finish.

So much for that less-than-one-hundred-pound, ever-busy "Martha" in my life.

MY SECOND MOTHER:
The "Mary"

— Chapter 9 —

But God did not stop there. He also sent me a second mother, in the form of a mother-in-law, whom I considered my "mother-in-love." She became the "Mary" in my life: the Senior Mrs. Ponder, whom I always called "Mother," too.

She entered my life when I was living "deep in the heart of Texas," far from the East Coast home of my childhood. Mamie Ponder did not rush about doing things for me. She let others do the outer things for both of us, while she sat quietly and comfortably in her big rocker, in a room filled with prolific green potted plants and a large picture window through which light flooded in.

HER CHARM-SCHOOL QUALITIES

There, in that room, she gave me her complete attention as she nurtured me with love and understanding. Although she had suffered much personal sorrow, she discussed none of it: whether having suddenly lost her beloved husband when he was only fifty, or one son at forty-five, or another son—my late husband—at age forty . . . all of massive heart attacks. She never discussed other family tragedies, either.

Instead, in the words of Dale Carnegie, she always spoke to me "in terms of my interest." She was a one-person charm school. She supplied me with unconditional love. Whatever bothered me bothered her. Whatever made me happy gave her great joy. She not only wrote me notes of love and appreciation, but from the time I married her son, she also tithed to my various ministries and continued doing so for the rest of her life . . . as tangible proof of her love.

HER FAMILY QUALITIES

At difficult times when I would otherwise have been alone (such as after the death of my husband Kelly); on holidays; after long, tiring, nationwide lecture trips; or after finishing the joyous but tedious task of writing a book, I always found comfort with the stout, matronly, motherly Mamie Ponder. Having been a student of inspirational thinking since the 1930s, she was my greatest cheerleader.

Sometimes I heard her say to people, "I often tended the card table filled with books for sale at church services in the 1930s. Little did I know that someday I would have a daughter-in-law who would write more books than that card table could hold!"

When she learned I was moving from Texas to California to continue my work, she cried—thinking she would never see me again. But through my return visits to Texas, I made sure we continued our joyous reunions at regular intervals.

IN MEMORIAM

Twenty years before her death, Mamie Ponder first asked me to conduct her memorial service. At various time over the years, even after I moved from Texas to California, I reassured her I would. When she quietly passed on one spring night at the age of eighty-nine, my son and I proceeded to plan her memorial service: he from Texas, me from Palm Springs—by telephone.

After I delivered my personal tribute of love to my mother-in-law, I continued with a "celebration of life" service. It began with an upbeat version of a well-known song of comfort and it ended with a familiar musical version of the Lord's Prayer. A profusion of colorful spring flowers perfectly matched the distinct colors of the adjoining stained-glass windows, through which the late-morning light streamed in.

Afterward, one attendee exclaimed, "What a glamorous service!" Of course, my son and I had deliberately planned it that way, feeling that Mamie Ponder deserved nothing less.

So much for my matronly never-doing, always-listening, ever-loving second mother—the "Mary" in my life.

MY THIRD MOTHER:
The "Critical Motivator"

— Chapter 10 —

In between those two "Southern ladies of the old school" was the mother who didn't love me, who didn't even want me—though I knew it not at the time. She was my first mother-in-law, and she turned out to be my severest critic.

Since she was also Southern, she had a great deal of pride. I was just a country girl in homemade dresses. She was sure I would never amount to anything and that I would be something less than an asset to the family. To all appearances, she was right.

HER MOTIVATING INFLUENCE

During much of the time I was married to her son, she lived downstairs in a big two-story house, in four rented rooms, so her circumstances were hardly more "affluent" than my own. She no doubt rejected me

129

because she hoped for a more successful daughter-in-law as a spouse for her only child—a natural reaction.

Not realizing at that point in my life that a person's severest critic can often be a great blessing in disguise, I nevertheless reacted with silent determination that I must prove her wrong—no matter how long it took. Though she was soon gone from my life, and later from this earth, her stinging criticism remained with me for many years. And it continually spurred me on toward much-needed self-improvement.

FORGIVENESS AT A DEEPER LEVEL

Fifty years later, I had—like most people who are fortunate enough to live fully—known both the triumphs and tragedies of life. I was having yet another difficult "learning experience" and realized I had to forgive and release at a deeper level than ever before.

At that point, I remembered my first mother-in-law, who had been on the next plane of life, as had her son, for many years. Since I knew that life is eternal and that people don't cease to exist just because they leave their body behind, I felt it imperative that I mentally talk to her about her having judged me so harshly. I wanted her to know she had thereby thrust me forth into a lifetime of constant physical work and inspirational studies, both of which had proved a necessity for my much-needed self-improvement, in emotional and economic ways.

It was time for me to say, "I FORGIVE YOU AND RELEASE YOU. I ASK YOUR FORGIVENESS AND

RELEASE FOR ALL THAT NEITHER OF US UNDERSTOOD
AT THE TIME."

A DIVINE COMMUNICATION

When I became quiet, called her name, began to
think about her, and pictured her as best I could remember, it was as though she came alive in my consciousness, and we communicated mentally and emotionally.

She seemed not only happy but also ecstatic to
have this contact with me. I mentally asked her to
forgive my youthful lack of understanding of the hard
life she had experienced before I knew her, which
doubtless had helped shape her attitudes toward me.

I reflected on what I knew she had gone through.
She'd had to divorce an abusive husband in the Deep
South in the 1930s, at a time when a divorced woman
was considered a social outcast. Abuse was acceptable and kept quiet. Divorce was not acceptable. She
had done the unthinkable, yet had survived to raise a
son alone. She had also lost a twelve-year-old
daughter to death by accident, and had supported an
aged mother for many years alone on a minimal income, with no financial help from her former husband.

No wonder she wanted her son to succeed and
have an affluent wife from a well-to-do family—credentials I certainly did not have.

THE UNEXPECTED BENEFITS

What she probably had not meant for evil at the time — only self-preservation — God had turned to good anyway. And I had not only survived, but eventually thrived as well. "You can now be proud of me" were my final words to her, as she faded from my consciousness, still smiling.

Would she have been as ecstatic and forgiving in our mental reunion had I not "made it" in her way of thinking? I do not know and I do not care. A hurt of fifty years' standing had been healed. What else mattered? "To err is human, to forgive divine." We both had erred, and we both had forgiven. A Divine communication had brought a compatible closure to our relationship — at last — fifty years later!

LESSONS IN LOVE
From My Three Mothers

IN CONCLUSION

So much for my three mothers: the one who loved me outwardly, the one who loved me inwardly, and the one who forced me to prove her wrong, thereby pressuring me to succeed. Perhaps my "critical motivator"—almost certainly without meaning to—had proved the words of Gibran: "Work is love made visible." Regardless of her original intention, was she among my greatest success motivators?

As I noted previously, "Love is not only 'a many-splendored thing,' but it can also be 'a many-splintered thing.' "

I trust that from these three women I learned the benefits of the various kinds of love they extended to me. And I know that over a lifetime they individually and collectively helped me to experience numerous of love's many-splendored, many-splintered aspects.

Whether I like it or not, they were three of my greatest teachers in life and in love. I trust that some-

133

thing from our mutual relationships will have been of
interest and inspiration to you.

oRder Dept
at
Renu Strauss

Maranda

See
A SPECIAL EXPLANATION
on the next page.

THAT GOLDEN SUNBURST

My readers have sometimes asked the meaning of the golden sunburst on the covers of my books. One commented: "When I see that gold symbol in a bookstore, I know a Ponder book is involved and I always check it out." Another reader said that's how she *finds* my books—by looking for that sunburst.

The symbol was not an original idea with me. It came from one of my publishers, the late Arthur Peattie of DeVorss & Co., who suggested that we use it on all my books for its beauty and as a symbol of distinction. His suggestion proved to become a popular one.

Here is its meaning, which ties in perfectly with the Wholeness I write about in all of my books: *In ancient times people of note often bore "seals" on their possessions as indications of their success and prominence. The golden sunburst found on the Ponder books is such a seal—one of enlightenment and abundance. Its fifteen points symbolize the breaking up of hard conditions and the expansion that enlightenment can bring—into one's royal heritage of increased health, wealth, and happiness.*

AN IMPORTANT NOTE
FROM THE AUTHOR

Through the generous outpouring of their tithes over the years, readers of my books have helped me financially to establish three new churches—the most recent being a global ministry, the nondenominational *Unity Church Worldwide,* with headquarters in Palm Desert, California. Many thanks for your help in the past and for all you continue to share.

You are also invited to share your tithes with the churches of your choice—especially those that teach the truths stressed in this book. Such churches include the nondenominational churches of Unity, Religious Science (Science of Mind), Divine Science, and others that are related, many of which are part of the International New Thought Movement. (For a list of these churches, write The International New Thought Alliance, 5003 E. Broadway Road, Mesa, AZ 85206.) Your support of churches such as these can help spread the prosperous Truth that humanity is now seeking in this New Age of enlightenment.

To contact Catherine Ponder or her UNITY CHURCH WORLDWIDE ministry for prayer help, literature, or other reasons, you may reach her at P.O. Drawer 1278, Palm Desert, CA 92261 USA.